Inclusive
PRACTICE IN
THE PRIMARY
SCHOOL

A guide for teachers

SARAH TRUSSLER
& DEBS ROBINSON

SAGE

Los Angeles | London | New Delhi
Singapore | Washington DC

Los Angeles | London | New Delhi
Singapore | Washington DC

SAGE Publications Ltd
1 Oliver's Yard
55 City Road
London EC1Y 1SP

SAGE Publications Inc.
2455 Teller Road
Thousand Oaks, California 91320

SAGE Publications India Pvt Ltd
B 1/I 1 Mohan Cooperative Industrial Area
Mathura Road
New Delhi 110 044

SAGE Publications Asia-Pacific Pte Ltd
3 Church Street
#10-04 Samsung Hub
Singapore 049483

Editor: Amy Jarrold
Associate editor: Miriam Davey
Production editor: Tom Bedford
Copyeditor: Audrey Scriven
Proofreader: Salia Nessa
Marketing manager: Dilhara Attygalle
Cover design: Wendy Scott
Typeset by: C&M Digitals (P) Ltd, Chennai, India
Printed in Great Britain by Henry Ling Limited at
  The Dorset Press, Dorchester, DT1 1HD

Library of Congress Control Number: 2014942071

British Library Cataloguing in Publication data

A catalogue record for this book is available from
the British Library

MIX
Paper from
responsible sources
FSC
www.fsc.org   FSC™ C013985

ISBN 978-1-4462-7489-7
ISBN 978-1-4462-7490-3 (pbk)

At SAGE we take sustainability seriously. Most of our products are printed in the UK using FSC papers and boards.
When we print overseas we ensure sustainable papers are used as measured by the Egmont grading system.
We undertake an annual audit to monitor our sustainability.

We would like to dedicate this book to Dr Felicity Fletcher-Campbell who has inspired us both and to our children: Jack, Harry, Lizzie and Martha.

CONTENTS

LIST OF FIGURES AND TABLES

Figures

Tables

ABOUT THE AUTHORS

Dr Sarah Trussler is a Deputy Headteacher at Woodlands Primary Academy, a larger than average inclusive school in inner-city Leeds. Sarah previously worked at Leeds Trinity University, where she was responsible for the training of teachers for primary education. Her research spans both of these fields, focusing on teacher attitudes to special educational needs and disability (SEND) and how students learn to work inclusively as they develop their early teaching skills. As well as being a Deputy Head, Sarah is responsible for inclusion in school, so understands the challenges faced by schools between an ethos of inclusion and funding, which is a key aspect of her research. Sarah is interested in embedding the Spiral Spectrum Model in practice to help improve teachers' understanding of the children they teach.

Dr Debs Robinson is a Senior Lecturer at the University of Derby and is a specialist in professional development for inclusive practice and SEND. She has had a long period of engagement in teacher education and provides initial teacher education (ITE) and continuing professional development (CPD) across the sector. She also works on non-ITE programmes focusing on social justice issues. Her background is as a primary teacher and special needs co-ordinator whose interest in inclusive practice was forged in her earliest experiences of working as a teacher in the inner London area. Her interest is in developing teacher education so that learners with SENDs may have their needs and rights better served by confident practitioners.

ACKNOWLEDGEMENTS

Sarah Trussler would like to acknowledge the support and inspiration offered by the students and school staff that took part in the research project leading to this publication. Sarah would also like to acknowledge the continuous support offered by her father, Tony, who created the spiral diagrams from our initial ideas.

Debs Robinson would like to acknowledge the support and inspiration offered by Pam Wooding and all of the colleagues that took part in the research project leading to this publication.

INTRODUCTION: HOW TO USE THIS BOOK

This book adopts the position that belief systems have a significant and lasting influence on how inclusive a teacher is likely to be. In other words, *the way we think about special educational needs, disability and inclusion has a significant impact on our practice, effectiveness and confidence.* Through examination of theory and practice, this book will help you to understand your own belief systems in ways that will inspire your development as an effective, inclusive practitioner. It will critique dominant beliefs about special educational needs and offer you alternatives that can support you in being more effective with diverse learners in the classroom. To support this, the book explores the research evidence about what makes some schools, classrooms and teachers more inclusive than others with reference to the implications of this for your professional development.

Each chapter includes carefully designed tasks and reflection points so as to help you to move forward in your practice and understanding. The beliefs, experiences and practices of real student teachers and experienced teachers will be presented to add detail to the concepts being discussed. These illustrations have emerged from the authors' own research combined with their extensive experience of working with student teachers.

Part One of the book explores the policy context, theory and practice of inclusive education. It then applies all of this to your development as an inclusive practitioner, providing practical examples and illustrations. The book proposes a new model of diversity called the *Spiral Spectrum Model.* The theoretical basis of this is introduced in Chapter 4.

Part Two of the book places more focus on the individual learners in your current or future classrooms and how you might understand and respond to their diversity and individual uniqueness in an inclusive way. The Spiral Spectrum Model is applied in Part Two so you can see how it can be used to bring about more inclusive outcomes for the learners in your class.

Each chapter or part can be read separately and non-sequentially.

PART ONE

CHAPTER 1

UNDERSTANDING SPECIAL EDUCATIONAL NEEDS, DISABILITY AND INCLUSIVE EDUCATION

Learning Objectives

After engaging with this chapter you will be able to:

- Understand what is meant by *inclusion*.
- Understand what is meant by *special educational needs* and *disabilities* (SENDs).
- Explain the tensions that exist between the terms 'inclusion' and 'special educational needs and disabilities'.
- Identify and reflect on your own belief systems about special educational needs, disability and inclusion.
- Reflect on your own stage of development as an inclusive practitioner.

Introduction

This chapter will explore what is meant by inclusion, and SEND. As you will discover, these terms are far from simple and there are different views about their meaning and value. Case studies of real student teachers will be shared, as a way of illustrating how these terms can be differently interpreted by professionals in the very early stages of their career. These illustrate varied stages of development in terms of preparedness and confidence for inclusive practice and you can consider how you compare. The chapter also includes a word-association exercise that will enable you to identify and reflect on your own belief system as this relates to special educational needs and disability, and this will help you begin the journey that this book has been designed to take you on.

Defining inclusion

It is frequently noted that the term 'inclusion' is hard to define. For example, Liasidou (2012: 5) describes inclusion as a 'semantic chameleon' because it adopts a different colour and meaning when used by different people, at different times, in different places. The following classroom scenario is presented as a means of reflecting on what is meant by inclusion and it will be returned to regularly during the discussion that follows.

Case Study: Dean and the science lesson

Dean (a 14 year-old with limited mobility) is in a science lesson in a mainstream classroom. The pupils are learning about electrical resistance. The teacher introduces the lesson and provides a well-structured explanation of the concept and how it links to previous learning. Practical demonstrations are used to support understanding. The teacher then sets a practical task where the students must measure the impact of variable levels of resistance on the performance of particular components. They are asked to collate and record their results and to draw conclusions. The students work in groups to carry out the experiment together. There is plenty of discussion between them. Dean is working one to one with a learning support assistant at a different table (of an adapted height so that he can draw his wheelchair up to it). He tells her what needs to be done and how he wants the equipment to be manipulated and moved (he cannot do this himself). He tells her what he wants recorded in writing. He makes progress with the task and the learning.

Dean says that he feels very included in this school and that he chose to attend it because it was the one he judged to be the most inclusive in the area. For example, he reports that he is included in science experiments (though they are not the best example of how he is included) and adds that the lessons he enjoys the most are ones involving group work and discussion. Dean gives the example of English where he was involved in lessons about debating in which people listened to each other and criticised each other's arguments.

Some people might argue that Dean's experience of the science lesson was inclusive because he was learning in the same mainstream classroom as his peers. Adjustments had also been made so he could participate equally in the learning and hence he made progress. In this way his impairments were understood and compensated for through adaption and support. Others however would say that this was *not* inclusion since Dean had been unnecessarily separated from other learners (in working separately with the learning support assistant). Though he had been included in the classroom he had not been included in the social community of the class and hence could not participate fully.

Dean himself feels included in science but probably feels more included in English because there is scope to work with his peers. Whilst we could be critical of the level of inclusion provided in the science class Dean seems to think it is sufficient, and from his perspective his experience of inclusion in the school is a positive one. This is an interesting illustration of how inclusion can be a matter of interpretation. It can also be a question of degree given that we might have an overall and general sense of being included (as Dean does), and the extent of this varies in different contexts (as Dean seems to recognise). For a number of reasons, inclusion is a difficult concept to pin down or be absolute about.

Arguably, it would be paradoxical to fix on a single definition of inclusion because our conception of it must be flexible enough to adapt to diverse and ever-changing people in diverse and ever-changing contexts. Darling-Hammond (2006) notes that the learner population is infinitely diverse and hence something we must be continually adaptive to. Further, what counts as inclusion for Dean on a Monday may not count as inclusion for Dean on a Wednesday, and what counts as inclusion for another pupil may not be the same as what counts for inclusion for Dean. This presents you with challenges as a teacher since it may make it hard for you to gain any consistent view of *what inclusion is* and *what you should be doing* as a demonstration of it. In terms of professional development, this implies that you will need to be reflective, flexible and adaptable in order to be an inclusive practitioner. This book has been written to help you navigate that challenge.

However, in terms of its broader principles and practices there is some consensus on what inclusion means. A definition provided by the Office for Standards in Education, Children's Services and Skills (Ofsted) (the school inspection body in England) is one example that will be analysed and built upon to establish what these principles and practices might be:

An educationally inclusive school is one in which the teaching and learning, achievements, attitudes and well-being of every young person matter. Effective schools are educationally inclusive schools. This shows, not only in their performance, but also in their ethos and their willingness to offer new opportunities to pupils who may have experienced previous difficulties. This does not mean treating all pupils in the same way. Rather it involves taking account of pupils' varied life experiences and needs. The most effective schools do not take educational inclusion for granted. They constantly monitor and evaluate the progress each pupil makes. They identify any pupils who may be missing out, difficult to engage, or feeling in some way to be apart from what the school seeks to provide. They take practical steps – in the classroom and beyond – to meet pupils' needs effectively and they promote tolerance and understanding in a diverse society. (Ofsted, 2000: 7)

This definition represents a number of common dimensions of inclusion as follows.

Inclusion is not just about SEND

The definition of an inclusive school presented above makes reference to the concern for *every* pupil (including those who may have special educational needs and/or disabilities). Hence, inclusion extends beyond SEND and is not just a term that describes the placement of learners who would otherwise have been in special schools into mainstream schools. Inclusion is a process that is concerned with everyone. Villa and Thousand (2005) consider inclusion to assume that every member of a school community has a right to belong and participate. This right is often extended to all stakeholders including staff and parents (Black-Hawkins et al., 2007; Corbett, 2001). If taking this perspective, Dean's experiences of the science lesson would fall short of inclusion since he could not participate with his peers and was separated from the community of the classroom.

Inclusion is a process that involves reflection, striving and positive action to counter inequality

Ofsted (2000: 9) note that the most effective schools 'do not take educational inclusion for granted' but strive to achieve this through a continual process of monitoring, adaption and improvement. This view is also adopted widely, often with particular attention paid to the way in which inclusion is concerned with an active commitment to removing barriers to participation (Sautner, 2008). With reference to Dean, though the barriers to learning were removed through the active allocation of teaching support and adapted furniture, it could be argued that the deployment of a learning support assistant actually created a barrier to participation since it enforced some separation of Dean from his peers and vice versa.

Inclusion celebrates diversity and adapts in response to diversity

There is also reference made to 'taking account of pupils' varied life experiences and needs' (Ofsted, 2000: 9), although other definitions are more likely to emphasise the importance of celebrating diversity and recognising it as a trigger for improving education for all (Villa and Thousand, 2005). Dean communicated something about his preference for group learning and discussion. If this had been heard, a different decision about how to use the learning support assistant might have been made in order to enact real respect for his 'life experiences and needs' (Ofsted, 2000: 9). Additionally, Dean's separation from his peers was preventing their enrichment. In this way, there may have been limitations on the extent to which this lesson reflected a concern to celebrate diversity and adapt respectfully to it.

Inclusion seeks to secure the participation of all members of the community in the full life of the community so that everyone can benefit

Ofsted (2000: 9) recognise that inclusive schools take note of who is not engaged or benefiting from the life and work of the school and act accordingly 'in the classroom and beyond'. This view of inclusion is widely supported. For example, Sautner (2008) notes that inclusion represents a proactive concern to secure equality and acceptance for all, and Barton (2003: 10) argues that it involves the 'politics of recognition' being concerned with who is included and who is excluded in education and in broader society. Inclusion is often conceptualised as an issue that must extend beyond education in this way. In the case of Dean, whilst his educational needs had been met in terms of the learning objectives for the lesson, his more universal human need to work alongside his peers was not being addressed. This could be seen as a failure of recognition since his *capabilities* (an ability to learn through discussion with others) were overlooked, with the focus being on his *impairment*.

Florian (2007) argues that while inclusion is conceptually fluid and difficult, it does have some stability in terms of the principles it represents.

Underpinning inclusive philosophy and practice is a concern with human rights, equality, dignity, and the right both to *participate in* and *contribute to* communities. Once that right has been acknowledged, it is not possible to pass off practices as 'inclusive' when they are not. Keeping such values in mind can help us design and evaluate inclusive practice. Their presence may also trigger a different evaluation of Dean's experience in the science lesson.

Reflection Point

Develop your own definition of inclusion: 'Inclusion is ... '

How does Dean's experience represent your definition in action? How inclusive was this lesson? How could it be made more inclusive?

Defining SEND

In England these terms are defined in policy and legislation. Section 20 of the Children and Families Bill (HMSO, 2014) presents the following definition of special educational needs:

1. A child or young person has special educational needs if he or she has a learning difficulty or disability which calls for special educational provision to be made for him or her.
2. A child of compulsory school age or a young person has a learning difficulty or disability if he or she—

   i. has a significantly greater difficulty in learning than the majority of others of the same age, or
   ii. has a disability which prevents or hinders him or her from making use of facilities of a kind generally provided for others of the same age in mainstream schools or mainstream post-16 institutions.

Special educational needs are thus identified when the child requires a level of provision in education, health or social care that is 'additional to or different from, that made generally for others of the same age' (Children and Families Bill, 2014, section 21: 1). This definition places some focus on difficulty and disability.

Legally then the term 'SEND' signals the right of pupils with learning difficulties and or disabilities to a resource that is *additional to or different from* that which is usually provided. Pupils labelled with SEND are those who have significantly greater difficulty with learning than their peers and/ or a disability that might hinder their access to educational opportunity. Though the definition of SEND seems to reflect a strong interest in rights, Slee (2010), Hart (1996) and Corbett (1996) consider this concept of SEND to be problematic given that it involves the comparison of some children with others, thereby reinforcing the presence of a norm. Corbett (1996: 15) regards it as devaluing with 'undertones of exclusion and stigmatisation'. Also problematic is the falsely scientific character of this concept given that an identification of SEND will depend on how criteria are constructed and interpreted by assessors.

For these reasons there are some tensions between this conception of special educational needs and the construct 'inclusion'. The following task is designed to enable you to access this tension for yourself, understand why it might exist, and manage it in ways that will support inclusive practice.

 ## Task 1.1   Free association exercise related to special needs, disability and inclusion

Copy the four headings shown below. Then under each heading write down five words that *immediately* occur to you:

1 Inclusion.
2 Individual learning needs.
3 Special educational needs.
4 Disabilities.

In the authors' own research about the development of inclusive practice and thinking (Trussler, 2011), student teachers recorded the following under each of the headings (see Table 1.1). You may wish to compare these with your responses.

Very generally, this cohort of student teachers were more likely to use positive, enabling and constructive words when considering *inclusion* and *individual learning needs*. However, the terms *special educational needs* and *disability* tended to trigger an intensified focus on deficits, impairments, and additional or 'special' support.

This is not surprising given that the legal definition of special educational needs operates the same kind of discourse in referring to 'significantly greater difficulty in learning', disability as a hindering factor, and 'special educational provision' that is different from or additional to that

Table 1.1 Responses from student teachers under each of the four headings

Inclusion	Individual learning needs	Special educational needs	Disabilities
• Special educational needs	• Need more help with an area of learning	• Mental development	• Physical or mental impairment
• Gifted and Talented	• Caring	• Dyslexia	• Impairment
• English as an Additional Language	• TAs	• Children who are not able to do what others can	• Unable to do something
• Teaching assistant (TA)	• Support	• Physical/mental	• Not able to do something
• All children should be given the same amount of support	• Extra support should be given for children who need added help	• Disabilities	• Physical or mental problem
• Meet needs	• One-to-one support	• Physical impairment	• Physical or academic
• Working together	• Taking groups out of class	• Different needs due to disability	• Inability to think/communicate in the normal way
• Differentiation	• Extra help	• Assistance	• Physical and mental disability
• Relationships	• Extra support	• Extra support	• Physical differences
• Varied curriculum	• Specialist help	• Support staff	• Problem
• No barriers	• Differentiate	• Special educational needs co-ordinators (SENCos)	• Physical e.g. wheelchair
• Ensuring everyone is involved	• Lesson plans	• One-to-one support	• Visual impairment
• Unique child	• Tailored	• Some children may need extra support	• Mental, medical
• Involvement in an activity	• Individual education plans	• Extra resources that may be needed	• If children find it harder to do something they may have a disability
• Allowing all to achieve	• Every child has individual learning needs and styles which need to be catered for	• Statement	
		• Children who need more help than others	
		• Attention	

(Continued)

Table 1.1 (Continued)

Inclusion	Individual learning needs	Special educational needs	Disabilities
• All abilities • Everyone involved • Everyone • Equality • *Every Child Matters* • Opportunities • No matter what race, sex, ethnic background, all individuals should be able to participate in all situations • Involved • Fairness • Involve minority groups • Schooling for all children • To fit in • All religions should be celebrated • Ethnicity groups • Behaviour	• Teachers should provide activities • Varied resources • The best way to teach someone • Catering for each individual child • Everyone is different • Children are all at different stages • Meeting everyone's learning needs • Type of learning • Learning in different ways • Unique • Visual, auditory, kinaesthetic (VAK) • Targets and goals • Success criteria • Recognising preferred learning styles • Supporting personal development	• Specialist help • Individual education plans • Planning • Individual learning • Differentiate • Individual abilities • Inclusion • social and emotional aspects of learning (SEAL) • Equality • Behaviour • Braille • Collaboration	• Support should be given to children who have disabilities • Something that should be noticed and supported • May need carer • Disadvantage • Extra support • Needs assistance • Extra provision • One-to-one support • TA/support assistant • Specialist provision • Special requirements • Wheelchair

(Continued)

Table 1.1 (Continued)

Inclusion	Individual learning needs	Special educational needs	Disabilities
• Learning • Fun experience • Parents and children	• How an individual learns • Achievable • The personalised – physical, intellectual, emotional and social needs • *Every Child Matters* • Inclusion • Plan, do, review		• Planning • Differentiate • Something which can prevent/affect a child's learning • Inclusive resources • Inclusion in sport • Empathise • Potential • Self-awareness • Inclusive • Access • Equal • *Every Child Matters* • Safety • Behaviour • Learning about it

which is usually provided (Children and Families Bill, 2014, section 20). However, this does create a potential problem which can be illustrated by the case of Dean and the science lesson described earlier.

The practitioners working with Dean seemed to focus on his *difficulties* which meant they may have overlooked his *capacities* (which were to do with his ability to interact with others in learning tasks). They also took little account of his view of what was most effective for his inclusion (working with his peers). Their focus on what *different or additional support* he needed led to the allocation of a learning support assistant which had the actual result of separating him from the community of the class in ways that, arguably, detracted from everyone's experience. The focus seemed to be on his 'special' needs rather than the needs that he might have in common with everyone else. There was also a focus on what needed to be *given* to compensate for his difficulties rather than on what he could *contribute*. In this way there exists a strong association between how we conceptualise special educational needs and the experience we offer to learners in the classroom. This idea is explored in theoretical detail in what follows.

Ways of thinking about SEND

The following represents a framework for analysing the belief systems that may come into operation when we are using the concepts 'inclusion', 'special educational needs' and 'disability'. A more detailed analysis of student teachers' responses to the free association exercise will also be presented in support of your own reflections and development.

Analysing these responses confirms that, broadly speaking, the terms *inclusion* and *individual learning needs* prompted a Transactional Model response and the terms *disability* and *special educational needs* prompted Functional Model responses (see Table 1.2). Overall, the responses were slightly more towards the functional. When the students were operating within a Functional Model they were often using single word labels – 'mental', 'impairment', 'medical' – but when they were operating within the Transactional Model they used phrases more related to the rights of children and how they could be enabled – 'allowing all to achieve', 'meeting everyone's learning needs', 'fair opportunity'.

While one concept (inclusion) turns us towards a Transactional Model, other concepts (special educational needs, disability) can turn us back towards a Functional Model and ways of thinking and practising that can

Table 1.2 A framework for analysing belief systems about SEND (adapted from Trussler, 2011)

Functional Model	Transactional Model
A Functional Model focuses on what is wrong with the learner, what they cannot do, and what special support (or intervention) needs to be put in place to compensate for (or correct) impairment.	A Transactional Model focuses on how the environment (classroom layout, attitudes, teaching approaches) interacts with impairment to construct (or deconstruct) learning difficulties and disabilities. The focus is on the potential and capabilities of learners and on how to remove barriers to learning and participation.
Sub-models of the Functional Model	**Sub-models of the Transactional Model**
Medical/Deficit Model	**Social Model**
<ul><li>Focus on impairment and incapacity.</li><li>Positions cause of difficulty or disability within learner.</li><li>Conceptualises learning difficulty or disability as a deviation from an ideal 'norm'.</li><li>Interventions focus on fixing or compensating for impairment.</li></ul>	<ul><li>Focus on the impact of environment.</li><li>Positions cause of difficulty or disability within the complex interaction between individual and environment.</li><li>Focus is on removing barriers in the environment.</li></ul>
Charity/Tragedy Model	**Capability Model**
<ul><li>Learning difficulty or disability is regarded as a personal tragedy.</li><li>Interventions focus on protection and amelioration.</li><li>Professionals as carers rather than educators.</li><li>Sympathy and pity.</li></ul>	<ul><li>Holistic focus that takes account of the capacities and potential of learners.</li><li>Teaching approaches build on what learners can do and what they are interested in.</li></ul>
Resource/Support Model	**Social-political Model**
<ul><li>Focus on what support or resources need to be given to a learner rather than on what they might be able to contribute.</li><li>Focus on different or additional resources rather than on how universal provision might be developed to include all learners more effectively.</li></ul>	<ul><li>Focus on equality and rights.</li></ul>

limit inclusion. As an inclusive practitioner, this tension will be one of the challenges that you will need to manage.

Case studies of student teachers and their development as inclusive practitioners

Two case studies of student teachers are presented below which cast light on the challenges and rewards of inclusive practice.

Task 1.2   Stories of development in inclusive practice

Read the case studies and consider the following:

- What definitions and conceptualisations of special educational needs, disability and inclusion do Abigail and Kathryn operate?
- What has helped Abigail and Kathryn to develop their skill and confidence as inclusive practitioners?
- What factors might be involved in making one of the student teachers more confident than the other?

Case Study: Abigail

Abigail was placed in a class of 30, 5 to 6 year-old children who were described by Veronica (Abigail's mentor) and Jane (their previous teacher) as a 'good class' who were not particularly challenging in terms of behaviour and diversity. This was with the exception of one child, Sophie, who was at an earlier stage of development than her peers. Sophie had special educational needs.

To Abigail, inclusion meant educating everyone together within the same class. As a pupil in school herself, she did not see inclusion in practice since those children who may have had learning difficulties or special needs were taught in different classes or even in different buildings. She believed that things had moved forward in positive ways but

(Continued)

(Continued)

that the move towards greater inclusion had brought challenges. In Abigail's view, 'special needs' was a term applied to those children who were developmentally behind to a severe or extreme degree. The term also brought to mind conditions that had associated medical facts and followed a diagnosis. Abigail knew that some of these conditions were difficulties she had never heard of and had long names. She was daunted by the prospect of them.

Abigail believed that the most difficult needs to meet were those that seemed extreme but were not yet diagnosed or confirmed as a particular type of learning difficulty or disability. This was the case for Sophie who was introduced to Abigail as 'an enigma' by her mentor. Abigail explained that knowing that Sophie had undiagnosed special needs did trigger panic about where to start and about what she should be doing. No one could provide clear guidance on this since there had been no confirmed diagnosis. It felt like a waiting game for everyone. Abigail believed that the situation would have been helped by some 'proper medical facts' about what was wrong and what should be done from other professionals, perhaps those she had heard about from outside the school.

Reflecting further on her placement experience, Abigail believed that she did discover some solutions to the challenges of meeting diverse needs and responding to Sophie. She said that these solutions were based on common sense. She used some small adaptations and these helped Sophie to stay engaged (such as using visual prompts). She also learned that it was important to find children's starting points by assessing these and observing them every day to get a sense of where they were. During her placement she came to realise that using day-to-day observation and discussing ideas with the teaching team were useful approaches. Making things up as they went along seemed to get them somewhere with Sophie in the end. Overall, however, she was dissatisfied with her own practice but at the same time could report on improvements on her relationship with Sophie: she also did not have specific evidence of the progress Sophie had made in her learning.

Abigail also explained that she had had a close working relationship with TAs during the placement. They provided formal and informal advice and feedback and she benefited from this. Abigail believed that it was important to be humble and to value feedback from all colleagues since teaching was a job in which you will never stop learning. She would always regard TAs as equals.

In considering her own professional future, Abigail does have some worries about special educational needs. One of these is that in her class

(Continued)

(Continued)

there may be children with, what she termed, 'extreme' or undiagnosed needs who are not getting extra support, and for whom there is little clear guidance about what is wrong and where to start. Another worry was that there might be children with extreme behavioural needs. Both of these occurrences could be professionally and personally exposing.

Case Study: Kathryn

Kathryn chose to undertake her placement in an early years class since this was one of the options available. Prior to this placement, Kathryn did not have much experience of this key stage and age group. She was placed with a class of 30 children, aged 4 to 5. She worked with an experienced mentor (Anna) and Geraldine (TA).

Kathryn felt very supported by Geraldine who was able to tell her what she needed to know about the children. She also provided support with locating resources in the classroom and saved Kathryn a lot of work in that respect. Geraldine's interest in circle time was something that Kathryn had also learned from, and Kathryn came to trust in Geraldine's judgement and knowledge of effective teaching and learning. She had learned a great deal from her. A significant realisation for Kathryn was that TAs knew the children really well, and that this expertise was very important and something that students should draw on:

> *' ... the TAs were probably the most important part of the class just because they know the children so well, they're outside with them while they're playing, they're always doing group work with them, um, yeah team work was another thing I learned this year, totally!'*

Working in an early years setting for the first time had brought new insights that Kathryn valued highly. Among these was the teamwork mentioned above:

> *' ... It scared me to begin with ... It terrified me! But the children ... it was as if they always had someone to go to. I think that was nice. Everyone knew what they were doing so it wasn't like the classroom was fragmented like it can be sometimes. All the adults knew what they were doing – all the children knew what adults*

(Continued)

(Continued)

> *were doing. I think this may have helped make their learning more continuous in a way, I don't know if that makes sense?'*

Kathryn explained that she had come to realise how central this continuity was for the children. It brought them security and it meant that all of the adults in the learning environment could use their collective knowledge to provide the right kind of responses for individual children in all sorts of ways. Kathryn explained that although the teamwork added an additional layer of challenge and complexity, this sharpened her teaching because she had to communicate with others about what the children were to learn, and in doing so, clarified this for herself. Kathryn had felt very well supported and buoyed up by this team environment but she had come to realise that the most important beneficiaries were the children. She had also learned that teamwork was a key tool for inclusive practice.

At the conclusion of her placement, Kathryn described other aspects of her development as an inclusive teacher. She had learned that it was possible to use children's starting points and interests as a basis for personalisation whereas in Key Stage 1 (ages 5 to 7) and Key Stage 2 (ages 7 to 11) the curriculum had dominated. In the early years there was a new way of working revealed to her.

Her view was that if you didn't give up you would get there in the end. For children and for her, failing was part of learning. Kathryn felt that it was important to embrace this idea and to have faith in yourself and the children's ability to progress. She had also learned that being an expert in your children was an essential resource for teaching inclusively. When asked how her placement experience might help her to meet the needs of children she might meet in the future she said:

> *'Um, really know them, absolutely, really know them. I set targets for one of them [David] but they just didn't work because it wasn't until the last two or three weeks of placement I thought "Oh this is why it is not working" and just really get to know how they think and they work, what they respond to and what they don't. So, it's getting to talk to them, getting to play with them, that would really help.'*

Kathryn reported that she had developed an improved ability to respond to children's individual needs and stages of development during this placement. She had come to trust her judgement more and gained improved confidence. She had also learned that personalisation must embrace social aspects as well as curriculum ones. Kathryn was able to give specific examples of the progress that individual children

(Continued)

(Continued)

had made as a consequence of close assessment and planning. She reported that she had learned to be more systematic about this.

For Kathryn, inclusion was about valuing all the steps in progress and all the starting points, whether they were planned for or not and whether they were what was considered 'normal' or not.

Kathryn had also learned about the importance of listening and responding to children and giving them choices.

When asked what her understanding of the term 'SEND' was, Kathryn made the following response:

'Um, I don't know really ... when I've got a child with SEN or a disability I don't particularly see them as any different anyway. I prepare different work for them, and perhaps in my first year I would have put a bit of a cap on what they could do, but I have learned that they're just as capable as anybody else at having a go at doing it. It's kind of that "have a go" philosophy again.'

You may have noticed that Abigail operated a Functional Model of SEND. Her focus was on diagnosis, deficits and support. She was daunted by the prospect of having to teach children with special needs in the future and still felt unprepared. She also located the expertise for special needs outside of the school and did not place much value on the skills she had developed in assessment and planning, describing these as 'common sense' and 'making them up as we went along'. This may be because she sees special needs as something that only experts can manage. She valued the team approach as well and saw this as an important aspect of inclusion.

Kathryn has more confidence than Abigail. Whereas Abigail sees the assessment and planning she engaged in as 'common sense', Kathryn sees these as key skills and is able to be precise about the impact she had on learners. She also values team work and has learned a great deal about trusting children's capacities and trusting her own capacities. It is possible to identify a Transactional Model in this case since she focuses on what children can do and how she can adapt. Kathryn locates expertise within herself and the teaching team and believes that inclusion is a project that she can manage.

These differences in levels of confidence and preparedness are due to a complex range of factors, including the class, the children, the stage of training and so on. However, the wider research data (Robinson, 2014) does support the theory that the students emerging from a placement with higher levels of confidence and skill were those who operated a

Transactional Model more strongly than a Functional one, though it must be noted that they did operate both simultaneously (this is explored further in Chapter 2). The more confident students were also more systematic about assessment and planning so they could identify positive outcomes – this gave them confidence. Teamwork and collaboration were also essential to success as was embracing a 'make it up as you go along' approach as a feature of professional skill. Later chapters will provide practical support in developing these skills.

Summary

This chapter has explored the idea that belief systems interact with practices in ways that may either *promote* or *demote* inclusion. It has introduced two key models of SEND, the Functional and Transactional models of diversity, and explained why we may be torn between both as a consequence of dominant ways of thinking about special educational needs and the policy context. The Transactional Model tends to be connected to philosophies and principles and most practitioners will expound this model. However, when it comes to the policy and practice of including learners with SENDs, the Functional Model comes into play in being part of the discourse associated with these concepts. Trussler (2011) argues that this may be a reflection of the tensions between ethics and practice.

Further resources

Children and Families Bill Factsheet available at: www.gov.uk/government/uploads/system/uploads/attachment_data/file/219659/Children_20and_20Families_20Bill_20Factsheet_20-_20Introduction.pdf

Children and Families Bill (2014) available at: www.gov.uk/government/uploads/system/uploads/attachment_data/file/219659/Children_20and_20Families_20Bill_20Factsheet_20-_20Introduction.pdf

Critique of the Children and Families Bill by the Independent Parental Special Educational Advice (IPSEA) organisation available at: www.ipsea.org.uk/AssetLibrary/News/IPSEA%20key%20messages-%20draft%20SEN%20provisions,%20Select%20Committee%20and%20Bill%20FINAL%2013.02.13.pdf

Critique of the Children and Families Bill by the Alliance for Inclusive Education (ALFIE) available at: www.allfie.org.uk/pages/work/press.html

CHAPTER 2

THE POLICY CONTEXT FOR SPECIAL EDUCATIONAL NEEDS, DISABILITY AND INCLUSIVE EDUCATION

Learning Objectives

After engaging with this chapter you will be able to:

- Identify the medical and social models of disability.
- Understand how these models may influence classroom practice.
- Understand the relevance of the dilemma of difference to inclusive practice.
- Understand why contradictions and compromises are part of the character of inclusive practice.
- Explain key developments in English and international policy for inclusive education.

Introduction

In this chapter, the policy context for inclusive practice will be introduced in ways that will help you understand how you might manage its rewards, challenges and contradictions in order to bring positive outcomes to the learners you work with. Contrasting models of SEND will be explored in more depth than in Chapter 1, specifically, the Medical Model (associated with a functional conceptualisation of SEND) and the Social Model (associated with a transactional conceptualisation of SEND). A highly relevant concept known as the *dilemma of difference* (Norwich, 2008) will be explained so that you can reflect on your own experiences.

Models of SEND

The Medical Model

When practitioners are operating a Medical Model, they bring the language and conceptual frameworks used by medics into the educational context. For example, learners who have been given the label of dyslexia may be described as 'suffering from' dyslexia, with dyslexia regarded as a condition experienced by people with abnormal neurological or cognitive functioning. More generally, the cause of difficulty is placed within the individual in terms of physical, cognitive, psychological, mental or neurological deficits in function. The following forms of language may be triggered when a Medical Model is in operation; diagnosis, condition, cure, remedy, treatment, abnormality, functional deficit, specialist, expert.

When operating a Medical Model, practitioners may prioritise specialised teaching approaches designed to remedy deficits or difficulties. For example, learners with Asperger's Syndrome may be trained to use particular social skills through the use of specialised behaviourist techniques where, in a clinical and controlled way, positive reinforcement is used to make particular behaviours 'stick'. This form of practice might then bring positive outcomes to the learner and prove to be the correct form of action. However, many would argue that the Medical Model will result in exclusive practices if over-applied (Parry et al., 2010).

Rieser (2001) argues that its operation leads to a focus on what is wrong with a learner rather than what is wrong with the teaching approach or wider education system. This fails to capture a holistic account of the interaction between the learner and the social world with the result that *fixing the learner* is emphasised above *fixing the education system*. Slee (2010) asserts that this model devalues and stigmatises learners, giving teachers false belief in the validity of labels and cures. Thomas and Glenny (2005) argue that a medical model has dehumanising effects and promotes among mainstream teachers the false impression that they are not qualified to teach all learners. However, there are some claims about the potential value and relevance of a Medical Model to the education systems and these are debated later in the chapter.

The Social Model

The Social Model arose from the disability rights movement during the 1970s and 1980s (Finkelstein, 1996; Oliver, 2000). During this period, disabled people were becoming increasingly resistant to the common practice of hospitalisation and institutionalisation on the basis that such practices were oppressive. For example, in 1972 Paul Hunt formed the Union of the Physically Impaired Against Segregation (UPIAS) with a mission to bring institutionalisation to an end so that disabled people could be full participants in their local communities.

When operating a Social Model, practitioners view the origins of disability and learning difficulties differently. Rather than situating this within the individual, they look to the environment to understand how teaching style, the curriculum, attitudes and the physical environment might be creating barriers to access and participation. For example, dyslexia would not be regarded as a deficit but as a natural human difference that only becomes a problem when teaching styles and curricular approaches are incompatible with the learning pace, preferences and capabilities of dyslexic learners.

There are criticisms of the Social Model. For example, if it were operated in a dogmatic way, it might lead practitioners to overlook simple, relevant or promising solutions. For example, a child might be having difficulty reading because they need glasses rather than because the reading material, teaching approach and attitudes of the teacher are at fault. It may also lead practitioners to avoid seeking labels or diagnoses even where these might be helpful in gaining additional resources or developing more positive learner identities (Riddick, 2012).

 ## Task 2.1   Identifying models of SEND

Read the comments below by student teachers and more experienced practitioners:

- Can you identify the medical or social models?
- What particular words, phrases or ways of thinking about SEND reveal these models?

Jane and Anna (experienced teachers and mentors to undergraduate student teachers)

During a discussion about special educational needs, Jane and Anna were reflecting on their own feelings and concerns about teaching children with conditions with which they were unfamiliar. Jane said:

'Well, the problem here is that for medical conditions we just do not have the training! Like Prader-Willi – we are not doctors but

(Continued)

(Continued)

equally, with say Kirsty [a child with very challenging behaviour in Anna's class] we don't even know what she has got so we can't even look that up in a book!'

During the same conversation and a few minutes later, Jane and Anna put forward the following argument:

'In our setting, because it's early years, we just don't have ability groups. So, really, this means that we don't think "well that child is SEN so they need something different", but what happens is the adults know what particular children need and work on these things all the time. So what we can't do with students really, is show them good "SEN" practice because we don't do that. We try to make sure the learning environment is inclusive for everyone and that every child has their needs met that way. We also have a can-do attitude and try not to put a ceiling on potential.'

Abigail (PGCE student on her first placement)

When talking about how best to prepare for special needs and related conditions Abigail considers what response she might make when informed of children's 'rare complaints' or diagnoses:

'Well, I think with a medical diagnosis you need to know what, I mean … people can throw in all sorts of long sounding, you know, lists of this, "this is a child and they have whatever it is", um, and if you come across one you've never heard before, you need to Google it just to get a heads-up! I mean there were children at the school with other syndromes I had never heard of but you make sure you have a quick look, you know, to see what it's all about, so at least you know what the problems are likely to be as they manifest them in the classroom.

'You've got to get to know the facts, you know, not an assumption, not an "I think this is this" and "I think this is wrong with her." You need to know if there is a problem there and if it's been diagnosed or whatever you've got, you need to know the facts and you need to know that from a professional, not just hearsay or a word of mouth like "I think this is this", or "so and so thinks that because she knows a child that was very similar." You can't make those assumptions, you can't label them like that, you've got to get proper, proper medical facts and then you can build on that.

(Continued)

(Continued)

If you've not actually had the experience of working with children with any particular need, it is very difficult, it's panic – what do I do, where do I start?'

Sascha and Selina (TAs working closely with student teachers on placement in the school)

Sascha and Selina are discussing how student teachers might be more prepared to work with learners who have the label of special needs. They had also been reflecting very positively on the progress Abigail had made but were concerned about how anxious she felt about 'special needs'.

Sascha: I think it helps student teachers not to be so hung up about special needs if they can recognise that all children have individual needs because each child is an individual. It is all about acceptance of every individual child and feeling comfortable with the fact that every child, whether they have special needs or not, is different and needs some bespoke kind of response. Day by day, different children will need different levels of attention and support.

Selina: I agree with that. Children are affected by the changes in their everyday life. So even if a child is not labelled with 'special needs' they can have a bad day and that can affect their learning. Rather than thinking that some children are 'normal' and children with special needs are not, I think student teachers would be helped by seeing ALL children as normal. In another sense, in real life there is no such thing as a 'normal' child.

Sascha: In a way, I think Abigail may have been affected by her fear of an 'abnormal' child with extreme needs in a way she didn't need to be. It was as if she saw these special needs like a 'Jack in the Box' and that their 'special needs' would jump out at her because they would be so alien and different that they would be beyond her. If she could stop thinking of children with special needs like that I think she would have been more confident. You just need to take every individual child, know them holistically, and then plan in ways that are responsive to them. I think she may have thought it was all much more complicated than that and become unnecessarily anxious and hung up about it.

You may have noticed that contradictory models were in operation among these students and teachers. Jane and Anna (experienced teachers and mentors) seem to be operating the Medical Model in the first comment since they emphasise the medical nature of 'conditions' and locate expert knowledge in the medical community. It is interesting to note that when they are operating a Medical Model it leads them to feel ill-prepared and inadequate for 'special needs'.

Just a few minutes later, Jane and Anna adopt a Social Model, noting that their learning environment is continually responsive to individual needs and that this includes those that may be labelled as 'special'. This anti-labelling, 'education for all' stance is a strong representation of a Social Model and we can see that these practitioners are using (almost simultaneously) contradictory discourses. In the first comment, a Medical Model is dominating, and in the second a Social Model is dominating. It is not unusual for practitioners to operate opposing discourses in this way. As has been noted in Chapter 1, the concept 'SEND' tends to activate deficit discourses that are not always compatible with 'inclusion', and this seems to be represented in the specific case of Anna and Jane who also imagine 'good SEN practice' to be something separated from the universally inclusive approach they espouse.

Abigail is using a strongly medical discourse, placing a lot of emphasis on 'proper medical facts' and 'rare complaints'. Abigail also locates expertise outside the school context and adopts the position that labels must not be applied unless the person applying them has a proper level of expertise. This is a reasonable position to take but adopting a Medical Model so fervently seems to lead Abigail to assume that the skills base for 'extreme' needs will never be in the thrall of mainstream teachers. Giving support to the negative relationship between a Medical Model and teacher self-efficacy is the fact that Abigail ended her placement feeling particularly low in confidence about her capacity to practice inclusively (Robinson, 2014).

Sascha and **Selina** (TAs working closely with student teachers on placement in a school) adopted a Social Model orientation, seeing all children as unique, capable learners and rejecting the concept of a 'normal' or 'abnormal' child. Their reflections lead them to believe that Abigail's lack of confidence arose from her fear of 'special needs' and her conceptualisation of children with this label as abnormal and hence beyond her reach.

Reflection Point

Reflect on your experiences on placement.

What models have you seen operating among the staff you work with?

In summary for this section, the characteristics of the Medical and Social Models of SEND have been explored and it has been noted that a social model emphasises the effect of the environment in constructing learning difficulties or disabilities, whereas the Medical Model emphasises within child factors.

The impact of the Social and Medical Models on practice

It has been argued in this book that the way we think about SEND influences our practice in strong and direct ways. Parry et al. (2010) support this view and argue that when a Social Model is in operation, children and young people are more likely to experience positive, inclusive outcomes whereas the operation of a Medical Model is likely to lead to exclusive ones. When asking student teachers and practitioners to consider the potential impact of these models on practice, they present a more ambivalent review of the possible benefits and detriments of the operation of these models. Before these are presented, you may wish to complete the following task.

   Task 2.2   The consequences of models of SEND for learners

If a teacher is operating a Medical Model, what positive and negative consequences for teachers and learners may be likely? If a teacher is operating a Social Model, what positive and negative consequences for teachers may be likely?

Table 2.1 presents responses from student teachers and other practitioners about the impact of models of SEND.

It could be argued that both models have the potential to trigger positive and negative consequences for learners. This is why practitioners may operationalise both in pursuit of the best outcome for children. For example, practitioners who have the role of co-ordinating provision for learners who have the label of SEND will operationalise medical discourses and emphasise deficits in order to secure scarce additional resources for their learners, even though this is a direct contradiction of their values. As a new teacher entering this context, it is

Table 2.1 Views on the potential consequences of models of SEND

	Medical Model	Social Model
Potentially positive consequences	• Research into particular conditions may cast new light on learners' experience and inform innovations in pedagogy that support the inclusion of learners	• Schools may become progressively more inclusive as they adapt to secure the participation and engagement of all learners including those with the label SEND
	• Identification or diagnosis may trigger additional resources and the support of professionals who have expert knowledge that can inform teachers' practice	• There may be a reduced tendency to stigmatise learners with the label of SEND
	• Identification or diagnosis may help a learner to develop a more positive identity	• There may be a reduction in the number of children identified with the label of SEND since the disabling impact of any impairment will be reduced
	• Knowledge and understanding of a 'condition' may inform practice in positive ways, including forms of differentiation that are closely tuned to learners' needs	• Schools will be more innovative and responsive to their local communities
		• Learners are more likely to develop positive identities
		• Learners are more likely to feel valued
		• A focus on what children can do dominates
		• Assessment is holistic and focuses on the child as a whole being
		• High expectations may prevail
		• The need for segregated forms of teaching and learning is reduced
		• Teachers will feel a stronger sense of self-efficacy since no learner is conceptualised as 'abnormal' or beyond their pedagogic range

(Continued)

Table 2.1 (Continued)

	Medical Model	Social Model
Potentially negative consequences	• Learners may be characterised as 'outside the norm' and marginalised or stigmatised • Teachers may feel some absolution of responsibility given that the cause of the difficulty is located within the learner and not in their practice • Teachers may develop weak self-efficacy locating the expert knowledge needed to support learners with the label of 'SEND' outside themselves • Learners may be separated and segregated until remedial teaching helps them to come closer to the norm • Learners may feel some absolution of responsibility for their own progress and learning • Learners' deficits may be the focus of assessment rather than their capabilities or potentialities • Learners may feel devalued and isolated from their 'normal' peers • Low expectations and limited opportunities may result from a deficit focus	• Practitioners may overlook simple or relevant solutions that involve remediating or correcting an impairment (such as wearing glasses) • Practitioners could not draw on useful sources of research and expert advice that may improve their pedagogy for particular groups of learners (such as those with the label of dyslexia) • Resistance to identification and diagnosis may not be in the best interests of learners and their families • Learners may absolve themselves of responsibility for their own achievement and progress

important for you to be aware of the dilemmas you may face in navigating these contradictions. However, it is often argued that the Social Model is the one most likely to bring positive, inclusive outcomes to learners.

Misconceptions about the Medical Model

In some ways the analysis of the positive and negative impact of a Medical Model presented in the previous section represents a misconception that it is important for you to be aware of. Teachers often argue that a Medical Model is still needed to ensure the full support of learners with SENDs since it is important to identify and understand impairment.

However, the social model can accommodate acknowledgement and the response to impairment. Individualised modes of support and intervention are not entirely discarded when it is in operation. Rather, the discourses of the Social Model encourage us to place more emphasis on *disability* and on the way in which our attitudes and practices might either magnify or minimise the disabling impact of an *impairment*. In this way we do not conceive the impairment as a disability. Rather, we consider the disability to arise from the interaction of the impairment with the environment. The real challenge is to recognise impairment at the same time as resisting discriminatory attitudes and practices. This can be hard to do and the essence of the challenge is well represented in the concept of the *dilemma of difference* (Norwich, 2008).

The dilemma of difference

Norwich (2008) describes the *dilemma of difference* in the following way. On the one hand, if we identify difference (through diagnosis for example) we run the risk of stigmatising and marginalising learners in ways that may limit their opportunities. On the other hand, if we do not identify difference and respond in the form of positive action, we run the risk of neglecting learners in ways that may limit their opportunities. Norwich (2008) argues that this is a perennial dilemma for inclusive practitioners and that it may demand of them some flexibility and compromise. The following task is an example of the management of dilemmas.

Task 2.3   Mediating the negative impact of labels

The following provides an account of Michelle's management of labels. What dilemma is she faced with and how does she manage this dilemma in order to secure positive outcomes for this pupil?

> Michelle has been employed by the school as a TA to support Christopher. Christopher has a statement of special educational needs because he has been diagnosed with Prader-Willi Syndrome. Michelle is reflecting on how important it is to understand Christopher's condition.
>
> Michelle said that for her the most important thing was getting to know Christopher. She explained that she had done some reading and research on Prader-Willi Syndrome but that she also knew that 'no child is a text book child'. She also commented that meeting with his mother was the most important thing because it put things into context since 'she told me exactly how it was for them'. She explained that the 'theory' of the condition had not applied much to Christopher yet. For example, he didn't forage for food (partly because he had been trained not to at home). She had also pondered on how the list of characteristics for the condition on the one hand didn't relate to him, but on the other, could have related to lots of other children in the class. She said 'For me, it was getting to know Christopher and getting to know his mum, meeting his family that was the most useful thing'. She also said that she thought that knowledge of the 'theory' might be relevant however, because behaviours like 'foraging' might emerge as he got older and she would know how to interpret that and what to do if it emerged.

Michelle seems to take a cautious but open view about the relevance of Christopher's condition, being willing to engage particular criteria (such as foraging) if and when they become relevant. Arguably, Michelle is adopting a position that will enable her to manage one of the dilemmas identified by Allan (2008) – how to understand impairment whilst avoiding disabling attitudes and practices. There is also some sense in which Michelle is aware of the potential 'power' of labels to impose a homogeneous and ill-fitting identity upon unique learners. She may be deliberately holding the 'condition' and its associated label at bay in order to minimise its potentially limiting consequences. However, she also recognises that at some point in the future, the label or condition may serve an important and useful function in understanding Christopher's development and responding to him.

As a teacher, you may be faced with similar challenges. In the specific case of labels, Riddick (2012) argues that labels are not in themselves a danger to inclusive practice. Rather, the extent to which they are beneficial or detrimental depends on how they are handled by practitioners and she recommends that 'wise labelling' is the way forward. You may need to learn to mediate the negative consequences of labels in the same way that Michelle has.

The policy context for SEND and inclusive practice

There has been a growing commitment to inclusive education in the international community and an accompanying concern to develop teacher education in ways that support preparation for diverse learners including those with the label of SEND (Englebrecht, 2013; UNESCO, 2009).

In England, policy developments have reflected a general move toward a Social Model of SEND (and away from a Medical Model) though there are still some tensions and contradictions arising from the desire to secure an education system that is more inclusive for all (i.e. about universal provision) and one that can secure positive action (sometimes in the form of additional resources) for those individuals or groups who need it. This indicates the way in which the dilemma of difference may play out in policy, and more importantly, how your work as a teacher is set within a context where contradictions in policy may lead to contradictions in your own practice that you will be faced with resolving. The next section explores the policy context for inclusive education. It sheds more light on how policy reflects prevailing belief systems about disability.

1913 Mental Deficiency Act

This act led to the development of four categories of mental deficiency. For example, 'idiots' formed one of these categories and 'imbeciles' another. These terms had psychological and scientific origins since they were used to describe grades of intelligence as determined by intelligence tests that were very popular at the time. The term 'imbecile' was applied to individuals with an intelligence quotient (IQ) score of 26 to 50 and the term 'idiot' was applied to IQ scores between 0 and 25. Those individuals falling into the 'imbecile' and 'idiot' categories were likely to be placed in a hospital or asylum or they would be required to be under the oversight of a parent or guardian. At this point it was believed that intelligence was hereditary and that education had limited impact. Hence, there was a fixed view of intelligence embedded in this legislation and the Medical Model was dominant given the focus on 'deficiency', labels and segregation. It reflected a dominant and mainstream philosophy known as Eugenics where it was believed that the human gene pool needed to be protected against defective elements. Hence, it was safest to separate defectives from the mainstream population so as to prevent them from reproducing.

1944 Education Act

In order to remove the language of 'defectiveness' and create an education system that accommodated diverse intelligences, this act introduced 11 new categories that could be used to ensure the right kind of education and care for particular types of children. These were: epileptic, deaf, blind, partially sighted, maladjusted, diabetic, delicate, physically handicapped, speech defective, and educationally subnormal. This legislation continued to reflect the trust placed in intelligence testing and the impact of heredity on pupil potential, since it proposed a tripartite education system that included grammar schools (for those children with the highest intelligence and potential), secondary modern schools (for those children with moderate intelligence) and technical colleges (for those children who did not have academic potential but who might perhaps thrive in more practical settings). An intelligence test (known widely as the 11-plus) was used to decide on the most appropriate destination for all children at the end of primary schooling. Children who were categorised as 'Educationally Sub-Normal' (ESN) were often in separate provision, and those categorised as severely ESN did not have a right to education but were the responsibility of the health authority. Despite a concern to accommodate a wider variety of learners through providing a more diverse set of educational placements, the Medical Model may still be seen as dominant given the concern with norms, categorisation and fixed models of intelligence. Intelligence testing was still being used as a basis for categorisation and decision making about which form of education would be suitable for each type of learner.

1970 Education (Handicapped Children) Act

This act was a significant turning point for inclusive education since it removed the category 'uneducable' from the system and imposed on local education authorities responsibility for all learners, including those who may have been given the label 'severely educationally sub-normal'. At this point special education grew as a movement given the proliferation of special schools and a related growth in the number of professionals working in this field (teachers, learning support staff, psychologists). Hence the research base for special education was associated with the scientific research tradition and special techniques were developed and tested in ways that were largely separate or distinctive from the educational research happening elsewhere. It can be argued that this is where the unhelpful separation of teaching and learning for 'special education' and teaching and learning for 'normal education' was established. As such it may have left a negative legacy, since mainstream teachers were led to believe that their knowledge of teaching and learning was insufficient and inadequate when it came to SEND (Florian, 2010; Thomas and Glenny, 2005). However, this legislation was a key milestone in securing the right to education even given that its concern to segregate learners with SEND from their local schools and communities has been strongly criticised (Ainscow, 2008).

1978 Warnock Report and subseque·
1981 Education Act

These developments in policy ar ·   ·nother milestone in inclusive education   ᵉ abolished and replaced with the umb.   ᵗls' and an accompanying concern to see   ᴜmething fixed and static. The aim was   ᴜout provision were focused on educational n.   .-educational ones (e.g. in terms of medical certific.   .ᴠas also a concern to minimise labelling and develop holi.   ᴜ of assessment that focused not only on impairments but also or. .ᴇngths, capabilities and preferences. Parents were also given more say in decision making, and placement in mainstream school was promoted as a default position, with some caveats. The Warnock Report (1978) and the Education Act (1981) represented a move towards a more inclusive system and the increasing influence of the Social Model.

2001 Special Educational Needs and Disability Act (SENDA)

In this legislation,/the rights of disabled children to placement in a mainstream school were strengthened slightly, albeit still with caveats related to resources and educational efficiency. The legal definition of special educational needs established in the 1996 Education Act was carried forward. This confirmed that children had *special educational needs* if they required provision that was *additional to or different from* that which was usually provided. In other words, the term 'SEN' was used to identify provisions that cost more. Different or extra provision was deemed to be necessary if learners had a *learning difficulty* that was significantly greater than other children of the same age, or a disability that hindered access to opportunities that were usually available. It made discrimination against disabled people illegal and emphasised the duty of all educational establishments (including further and higher education) to make reasonable adjustments in order to secure equal opportunities and eliminate discrimination. Hence, it placed some emphasis on barriers in the environment and reflected a Social Model.

However, there are tensions here since many would argue that the definition of SEND embedded in this legislation continues to place the source of the difficulty within the individual, with an ensuing tendency to promote deficit discourses about difficulty and disability (as discussed in Chapter 1). This act avoided any other form of categorisation. The SEN Code of Practice (DfES, 2001: 85) also avoids hard and fast categories of need although it does present four areas: communication and interaction; cognition and learning; behaviour; emotional and social development; sensory and/or physical. It is also noted that children may have difficulties across more than one area. Hence, SENDA (2001) and the SEN Code of Practice (2014) seem concerned to move away from categorisation and labelling in an attempt to construct a more flexible and humanising conception of SEND.

It has been argued that the definition of SEND used in policy has been designed to inform decision making about who should get the more costly provision and who should not (Slee, 2010). Those children whose learning difficulties are more exceptional should receive provision that is more exceptional. However, Robinson (2014) found that this policy causes tensions. Most notably, practitioners report that where a child has a label that arises from the medical or psychological community (e.g. Down's Syndrome, Prader-Willi Syndrome, cerebral palsy) this has more resource-garnering power than labels that are less bounded and 'scientific' (such as emotional and behavioural problems, general failure to progress) and this point is also supported by Peer and Reid (2012). In this way, while policy may be demoting categorisation and labelling and promoting a Social Model of disability, practitioners know that they must pursue labels and medical forms of diagnosis in order to secure resources. They also know that they must emphasise children's deficits rather than their capabilities.

Removing Barriers to Achievement (DfES, 2004)

This strategy for special educational needs set out the Labour government's vision for inclusion. It demonstrated a strong commitment to inclusive education and to its principles:

> All children, wherever they are educated, need to be able to learn, play and develop alongside each other, within their local community of schools.

It followed the Green Paper *Excellence for All Children: Meeting Special Educational Needs* (DfES, 1997) and the subsequent *Programme of Action* (DfES, 1998), and promoted the importance of personalised learning and of practices that would be more responsive to the needs of diverse learners including those with special educational needs.

This policy adopted a strongly Social Model, noting the importance of early intervention and of the proactive removal of barriers to learning. It also placed more emphasis on accountability since teachers and schools would be required to sharpen their focus on the progress made by children with special educational needs. The legislative framework for the Green Paper *Every Child Matters* (DfE, 2003) was connected to this strategy, since it focused on multi-agency working, joined-up services, and the need to ensure that all children and young people could experience positive outcomes in their education and beyond.

2014 Children and Families Bill

This legislation was pre-empted by the Green Paper *Support and Aspiration: A New Approach to Special Educational Needs and Disability* (DfE, 2011). The concern was to give parents a real choice of school, with the government stating that 'we will remove the bias towards inclusion' (DfE, 2011: 5). The coalition government were concerned that placements in mainstream schools were being forced on families and that these w⌣. not necessarily the best option. They were also concerned that the system was overly complex and that families were having to battle through bureaucracy in order to access the right support for their children.

The Children and Families Bill (2014) emphasised the importance of positive outcomes for children and young people with special educational needs with reference to health, education, employment and independent living. For example, clause 20 notes the responsibility of the Local Authority to 'facilitate the development of the child or young person to help him or her achieve the best possible outcomes'. The bill also extended provisions from ages 2 to 16 (as had been established in SENDA, 2001) to birth to 25 in order to provide better support into adulthood. Local Authorities will be responsible for creating a single education, health and care plan so that different services can work more cohesively and reduce complexity for families. There was a requirement for improved co-operation between these services. Parents were also to be given a personal budget in order to secure more choice and control, and Local Authorities were required to publish a local offer which provided an outline of the services available. Schools and colleges were required to ensure that children and families were as included in decision making as much as possible. All teachers were seen to be responsible for special educational needs and would be more accountable for demonstrating positive impact and progress for learners with special educational needs. The legislation applied to all schools including free schools and academies.

The definition of special educational needs and disability remained unchanged from SENDA (2001), and children with special needs and/ or disabilities were secured the right to an inclusive education (meaning admission to a mainstream or post-16 institution) unless this was not in keeping with the wishes and choices of children, young people and their parents, or unless it would disrupt the provision of efficient education of others. The right to a mainstream education was neither reduced nor strengthened. However, while the enhanced rights for children, young people and their families have been welcomed, the act has been widely criticised for the extent to which it might encourage movement of children with special educational needs from mainstream to special schools. This is because special schools will be able to admit children and young people without a statutory assessment, education, health and care plan, or a right to have the placement reviewed by an independent tribunal (Alliance for Inclusive Education, 2014). Where free schools and academies are establishing specialist provision, they would now be able to transfer children from their mainstream sites to special provision without due process. Though the desire to remove the bias towards inclusive education has not been explicitly stated in the bill, its regulations may result in an increasingly segregated system. Alternatively, a focus on the rights of children and young people to access the best possible outcomes may bring a more holistically inclusive experience for this same group. All of this remains to be seen.

In summary for this section, there has been a continuing shift towards a Social Model in policy and legislation. There has also been support for the principle of inclusive education, both in terms of its broader concern to create a more responsive education system for all learners and in terms of its concern to increase opportunities to access mainstream schooling, although the most recent legislation seems to take a more ambivalent view of this. However, there are also tensions. These relate to a sustained policy commitment to high stakes assessment and to the dilemma of difference. The following represents how practitioners may experience such tensions in their day-to-day work and it will help you to reflect on your own professional situation.

 Task 2.4   Tensions caused by resources

Consider the following comment by Alison (who is a special needs co-ordinator and who has a strong commitment to inclusion) and Lorna (a PGCE student teacher on placement in Alison's school who also shows a strong commitment to inclusive practice and strong abilities in this area). What tensions are these practitioners describing? Have you heard these tensions discussed in your placement school?

Case Study: Alison and Lorna reflecting on resource tensions

'I have [x] year old twins in the nursery at the moment who are not out of nappies and whose language development is at a really early stage. We are doing our best for them but we have to fund TA support ourselves and that is a huge chunk out of our budget. I mean, what am I going to do? We can't fund the speech therapy they need! We can't even fund the TA really, so that means that other children do not have a resource they would otherwise have had as we divert more and more hours to our twins ... sometimes it is a poisoned chalice being a school that is so good at inclusion, because we end up pushing our resource to the limit and it is the effect on staff and other children that worries me.'

(Continued)

(Continued)

Lorna associated the term SEND with needs that were 'severe', or 'extreme' and that resulted in the allocation of additional support. One of her worries for the future was having children in the class with more 'severe' needs who did not have this allocated support because they did not have a label:

' ... when their needs are not, um, as severe as someone who perhaps gets additional help all the time but they still cannot participate fully in the activities that a lot of the other children are doing, and I think those are the most challenging ones and the ones that I had in my class were like that, apart from Christopher who I didn't actually focus on for my Personalised Learning Plans (PLPs) because he already gets loads of support anyway. The others were at such a level like Skye and Danny who needed a lot of support but they are not classed as anything, so they have no statement but they do need somebody sitting with them to support them.'

Alison is expressing the problem she faces in keeping her values alive in a context where the wellbeing of staff and children may be compromised. The issue of resource allocation was troubling Lorna, and while she came to see inclusive practice as a manageable project (and one that this placement had prepared her to undertake), she was concerned about the impact of insufficient support on her capacity to reach all children. Armstrong et al. (2010) note that though policy seems to promote inclusion, beneath the surface is a more powerful interest in the financial control of resource distribution. This gives permission for less and less investment and hence limits the progression of a truly inclusive system.

Summary

This chapter has explored the exciting, dilemma-filled and contradictory policy and practical context for inclusive education. Examples of policy illustrate the manner in which practitioners must manage contradictory priorities and discourses. For example, although teachers may want to spurn labels and their devaluing effects, they will also sanction them if this is likely to bring positive outcomes for children. As a teacher you will need to manage these contradictions as well as identify when different discourses are at work and how you might operationalise these to support inclusive education.

Additional resources

A useful timeline covering disability history (and key pieces of legislation) is available at: www.breakthrough-uk.co.uk/Resources/Breakthrough%20UK/Documents/Policy/disability-history-timeline-2013.pdf

The original Green Paper that launched the Children and Families Bill is available at: http://webarchive.nationalarchives.gov.uk/20130401151715/https://www.education.gov.uk/publications/eOrderingDownload/Green-Paper-SEN.pdf

The Young Person's Guide to the Children and Families Bill is available at: www.gov.uk/government/uploads/system/uploads/attachment_data/file/189968/Young_person_s_guide_to_the_Children_and_Families_Bill.pdf

CHAPTER 3

MODELS OF DIFFERENCE AND DIFFERENTIATION

Learning Objectives

After engaging with this chapter you will be able to:

- Understand the relationship between a positive professional identity and becoming a confident, inclusive teacher.
- Evaluate the helpful and unhelpful effects of a Normative Model of difference.
- Understand the Spiral Spectrum Model of difference.
- Explain your personal approach to modelling difference in your classroom.
- Choose from a range of starting points for differentiation.

Introduction

In this chapter the importance of a positive professional identity will be explored with reference to two student teachers, Abigail and Lorna. Different ways of thinking about diverse learners will also be reviewed, starting with the 'Normative Model of difference' and then moving to an alternative model, the 'Spiral Spectrum Model of difference'. Finally, alternative starting points for differentiation will be outlined with reference to how these might trigger more inclusive ways of planning and teaching.

Starting with you: professional identity and SEND

In previous chapters we have explained why *the way we think about SEND influences our practice* in strong and direct ways. We would also argue that *the way we see ourselves as professionals* will have an impact on our confidence and for SEND. The following is a case study of a student teacher, Abigail, during her first placement and is presented as an example of this. (The fuller case study was presented in Chapter 1, on page 17.)

Case Study: Abigail's conceptualisation of SEND

For Abigail, the term 'SEND' carried a lot of weight. In her view, SEND was a term applied to those children who are developmentally behind to a severe or extreme degree. It also brought to mind conditions that had associated medical facts and followed a diagnosis. Abigail knew that some of these conditions were things she had never heard of and had long names. She was daunted by the prospect of them.

She believed that the most difficult needs to meet were those that seemed extreme but were not yet diagnosed or confirmed as SEND. This was the case for Sophie (a child in Abigail's placement class) who was introduced to Abigail as 'an enigma' by Veronica (her mentor and the class teacher), since she and her previous teachers had not been able to get to the bottom of what the problem was although they had been informed that it was something to do with language processing. Generally, Abigail found Sophie perplexing and was not alone in this. Four members of the school staff (Veronica, Elaine, Jane and Sascha) had perceived in Sophie a spiky profile, meaning that she seemed competent in some areas (like number work) but was struggling in others (such as receptive comprehension). Veronica and Jane confirmed that they had developed a strong affection for Sophie but had been similarly perplexed on occasion. Working with Sophie had not been without its intermittent frustrations for that reason and both teachers believed that it was important to understand this before making any judgements about Abigail's competence.

Abigail explained that knowing Sophie had undiagnosed SENDs did trigger feelings of panic about where to start and about what she should be doing. No one could provide clear guidance on this since there had been no confirmed diagnosis. It felt like a waiting game for everyone. Abigail believed that the situation would have been helped by some 'proper medical facts' about what was wrong and what should be done from other professionals, perhaps those she had heard about from outside the school:

(Continued)

(Continued)

'You've got to know as much as you can about them, you've got to get to know the facts, you know, not an assumption, not a "I think this is this" and "I think this is wrong with her". You need to know if there is a problem there and if it's been diagnosed or whatever you've got, you need to know the facts and you need to know that from a professional, that it's not just hearsay or a word of mouth like "I think this is this" or "so and so thinks that because she knows a child that was very similar". You can't make those assumptions, you can't label them like that, you've got to get proper, proper medical facts and then you can build on that ... '

You may identify here with Abigail's fear and anxiety about SEND and you may also have seen and heard this among other practitioners in your setting. I felt just like Abigail in my early career and tended to believe that I would never have the expert knowledge I needed to 'do the right thing' for learners with a label of 'SEND'. The fact that there was a TA working with me and watching me day after day added to my feelings of inadequacy. When we find ourselves in this position, it is natural to assume that there are others who have the expertise and knowledge to do a better job.

However, it is important to adopt a positive *professional identity* when it comes to SEND. While it is right and proper to acknowledge that there are other professionals who can help us improve our practice, it is also essential to understand that when teachers see themselves as professional, with *valid professional knowledge and skills in SEND*, rather than inadequate amateurs who are dependent on 'experts', they are more likely to take on the challenges of inclusive practice. It is important for teachers to understand and recognise the *particular skills and insights* they can bring to the *particular context of the classroom*. Confidence and self-belief are vital traits in an inclusive teacher, as has been demonstrated in research about the relationship between teacher identity and professional efficacy for SEND. For example, some early research by Sarason (1990) revealed that teacher preparation programmes in the USA had created a particular conception of preparedness for diverse learners. Graduates emerged believing that there were two types of human being (those with SENDs and those without) and that choosing to work with one type rendered you incompetent and inadequate in working with the other type. Sarason (1990) suggested that diverse learners might be better served if initial teacher training had been structured to promote a readiness not for a particular age or type of pupil but for *all* learners. Further, Kearney (2007) reports that in the case of disabled children who had been marginalised from mainstream education, teachers had tended to assume permission to absolve themselves from responsibility for those children on the grounds that they were insufficiently trained or did not have the resources to cope.

Essentially, there is strong evidence to support the argument that where teachers identify *within themselves* relevant skills and knowledge for SEND, they are more likely to take responsibility for all learners and also more likely to secure positive inclusive outcomes. This is reported widely in the research literature (Campbell et al., 2003; Lambe and Bones, 2006). The following task explores this in more detail.

 ## Task 3.1   Constructing a positive professional identity for SEND and inclusive practice

Read the following case study of Lorna (a PGCE student). Though she had found the process of meeting the needs of diverse learners challenging, she does seem to have emerged from the placement with higher levels of confidence than Abigail. What do you notice about how she evaluates her own skills?

Case Study: Lorna's conceptualisation of inclusion and SEND

To Lorna, inclusion meant educating everyone together within the same class and she had come to believe, from her experiences during placement, that this was possible. For her the term 'SEND' related to children who may have more severe needs and have been allocated additional support.

Lorna learned that it was very challenging to meet diverse needs. This extended beyond planning for groups and involved planning very specific adaptations for individuals. The most challenging needs to meet and plan for were among those children who were struggling but were not identified as having SENDs and so did not have allocated additional support. There were a number of children who were in this position in Lorna's placement class.

There was clear evidence that Lorna did meet the challenge and she developed some important professional skills and perceptions that she believed would be transferable into her next placement. She valued these. Her understanding of how to personalise learning had developed and brought rewards. Key among these rewards was seeing tangible

(Continued)

(Continued)

evidence of children's progress and developments in their self-esteem as learners. She could demonstrate this progress with clear evidence arising from assessment. Selina and Sascha (the TAs working with Lorna during her placement) and Elaine (her mentor) also confirmed that Lorna had made an early, determined start in knowing children's needs and providing for these. She was committed to doing so from the outset and strove to find ways to include everyone.

During the placement, Lorna developed pedagogic approaches that had a positive impact on children's progress and inclusion (such as breaking things down into smaller chunks or designing simpler tasks). She came to understand that this depended on really knowing children's starting points and how they were likely to see things. Finding children's starting points through day-to-day observation and assessment was a vital step towards undertaking planning that would meet their needs. To Lorna, it seemed essential that teachers should become experts on all of the children in their classes as soon as they possibly could. She was beginning to think about ways that she could achieve this at the start of her next placement because she wanted to ensure that children continued to move forward in their learning. If they took a backward step because she was planning poorly matched learning experiences, this would feel disastrous. Hence, this became an absolute priority for her next time around.

The task she had to carry out in school (known as the Personalised Learning Task) was an important scaffold for learning how to personalise for individuals in a whole class environment in her view. Knowing the focus children well led to pedagogic adaptions that benefited the whole class, including those who were working at an advanced stage of development. Lorna believed that the Personalised Learning Task kick-started the process by which she learned to personalise. The early successes she had were motivating and she learned from these. Without the early focus on individual needs (as required by the task) she believed that her journey would have been slower and that she would have achieved less in terms of meeting individual needs. The children may have benefited less too.

Lorna also noted that in the school there was a strong commitment to meeting all children's needs. She felt included in the team and valued. Together Lorna and the team worked towards making sure that children's wellbeing and progress were secured. She had a close working relationship with the TAs and she believed that this benefited children directly because it brought continuity of experience.

Lorna gained from the expertise within the school and from the team's commitment to supporting students' learning generally and in

(Continued)

(Continued)

the area of SEND and inclusion. Her professional development felt like a priority in the school. As a result of this placement she had developed awareness and professional skill in the areas of inclusion, SEND and differentiation that she felt were suitable to take into her next placement.

Her only worry was that as a full-time classroom teacher, she would not have the time to become as expert in every individual as she would like. However, she was reassured by her experience of working with the TAs. Their knowledge and insight into the children's needs could compensate for teachers' lack of time. She had come to value their insight and to recognise this as a resource for personalised planning.

Lorna is able to describe the skills and insights she developed. She is also able to see their transferability to her next placement. It seems very important to Lorna to celebrate that she was learning to use assessment and in-depth knowledge of individual children as a basis for planning appropriately matched learning experiences. She also seems to have taken responsibility for this from the start. Her colleagues reported that she had been effective in this respect also and attributed this in part to her mentor's philosophy and expectations. Interestingly, Abigail reports that she had developed similar skills and insights about assessment, teamwork and pedagogic adaptations. She saw these as 'common sense' and was not sure that they were transferable to meeting the needs of children with exceptional needs. Lorna however (along with other students who reported developments in their confidence and readiness for SEND) conceptualised these as professional skills that were transferable to all children including those with SENDs. It could be suggested that there is a link between Lorna's professional identity and her effectiveness as an inclusive teacher.

Developing a positive professional identity for SEND is not an easy or straightforward thing to do. Some experienced teachers find it difficult to attain. Part of the solution lies in being dexterous and flexible about the conceptualisations of SEND that you adopt. The following section explores dominant and alternative ways to conceptualise difference and will consider how some approaches might be more supportive of professional self-efficacy for SEND than others. This adds to the discussion of the medical social models of SEND that were discussed in Chapter 2.

In summary, it has been argued that the route to inclusive practice includes the adoption of a positive professional identity for SEND.

Critiquing the Normative Model of difference

Arguably, the Normative Model of difference is dominant within our education system (Florian, 2007; Hart et al., 2004). This model is based on the statistical image of the bell curve as represented in Figure 3.1.

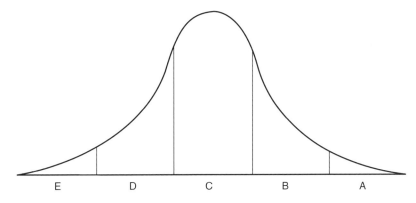

E   D   C   B   A

Figure 3.1   A bell curve representing normal intelligence

The 'norm' is identified through a process of quantitative data gathering where specific characteristics within a large sample of individuals are measured and the results plotted in frequency graphs. This commonly results in a bell curve with the *most* frequent outcomes in a population lying in the central range (C), *relatively frequent* outcomes lying either side of this (D and B), and the less common outcomes lying in the outer range (A and E). Outcomes in the central range are then conceptualised as 'normal' within a population, with C being 'the norm'. Outcomes lying further and further from the norm are considered to be more and more deviant or 'abnormal'.

This statistical concept is applied in a number of contexts. For example, during their babyhood and early years, children's weight, body length and head circumference are measured and plotted onto a graph representing the normal distribution for these characteristics. For example, when my first daughter was born her body length was plotted onto the 15th centile. This meant that 85% of babies had a body length longer than hers. Hence her body length deviated from the norm to a significant degree. However, her head circumference was on the 99th centile which meant that only 1% of babies had a head bigger than hers. This meant that her head circumference deviated from the norm to a very significant degree. This led to some follow-up medical investigations. It turned out that her parents and grandparents had unusually large heads too and so there was nothing to worry about. (I wished that someone had warned me about this before I gave birth!) In this way, the Normative Model is used to identify potential diseases or defects in medical contexts to direct treatments or therapies. However, it is also used in educational contexts, sometimes inappropriately.

Figure 3.1. represents the normal bell curve for intelligence. When psychologists design tests or assessments to measure IQ they trial them across a large sample of individuals and plot these on a frequency table to establish which results are most common (or normal) within a population and which results are uncommon (or deviant) within a population. For example, in the Standford-Binet Scale (1922) and the Weschler Intelligence Scale (2001) an IQ of 100 represents the norm. An IQ of less than 70 is significantly deviant from the norm and represents abnormally low intelligence. An IQ of more than 120 is significantly deviant from the norm and represents abnormally high intelligence. These tests are sometimes used to identify SENDs such as ADHD and autism. However, the reliability of these tests is much contested (Deary et al., 2010).

Arguably, the bell curve representation of diversity is somewhat dominant in educational contexts (Florian, 2007). Hart et al. (2004) are critical of the validity and impact of bell curve thinking in education. They argue that the Normative Model of intelligence promotes a fixed model of ability that limits teachers' and learners' beliefs in their capacity to progress. Most importantly, a fixed model of ability promotes the belief that teachers cannot make a difference to young people's future development. This limits their self-efficacy and willingness to transform their practice in response to diversity. Hart et al. (2004: 166) urge teachers and the education system to adopt the concept of 'transformability' in place of ability labelling or Normative models, with this defined as 'a firm and unswerving conviction that there is potential for change in current patterns and achievement and response, that things can change and be changed for the better sometimes even drastically, as a result of what happens and what people do in the present'. By this, the authors are emphasising the value of adopting fluid models of ability and potential. You may wish to reflect on what implications this has for your professional development.

 Reflection Point

What impact might the Normative Model of diversity have on our attitudes towards children with SENDs?

How might this impact on classroom practice?

There are a number of reasons why the Normative Model is not always the most helpful conceptual basis for inclusive practice:

- It might lead us to label children who differ from the majority as abnormal or deviant. In this way they can be devalued or separated in ways that are not supportive of inclusion. Children who are perceived as outside may be conceptually positioned as marginal outsiders or outliers with exclusive consequences.
- The Normative Model can lead to a *majority first approach*. In practical terms, this is a model of differentiation that *prioritises the majority* in planning appropriate learning experiences. Thereafter there is some tinkering at either end of the 'ability' scale to fit those who are in the minority. Black-Hawkins and Florian (2011) are particularly concerned about the dangers of a majority first approach since it means that the education system never has to innovate or transform to include all learners. In this way, it continues to favour the majority over the minority in ways that are incompatible with inclusion or social justice.
- The Normative Model represents one dimension of diversity. However, individual children are richly and deeply unique. If we take 'ability' as the dimension under consideration, we must recognise that this is variable across time, contexts and subjects. It is even variable within subjects. For example, some children may write fiction more ably than non-fiction. Their grasp of spatial maths might be much stronger than their grasp of number problems. Further, while a child may have autism, the impact of that autism may be less when that child is working with skilful teachers and more when working with less skilful teachers. The normative conceptualisation of difference cannot capture this diversity or complexity in ways that inform responsive teaching.
- As argued by Hart et al. (2004), the Normative Model can promote fixed views of capacity and low expectations of learners by teachers. It also reduces the self-efficacy of teachers since they may not believe in their capacity to transform the potential of learners, believing that their abilities are fixed.
- It is likely that learners with SENDs would be conceptually positioned in lower quartiles of the bell curve. Teachers are likely to have been successful in the education system and hence occupy the upper or 'normal' quartiles. This may lead them to see themselves as spatially distant (and hence professionally distant) from them. Therefore, as in the case of Abigail (the PGCE student considered earlier), everyday practices may come to be seen as irrelevant or inadequate in meeting

the needs of such 'extreme' or distant learners. Teachers may also come to believe that learners with SENDs are unreachable outliers that cannot be supported by the effective pedagogies that they already use and understand.

However, it has to be recognised here that this model of difference is still very influential in schools and often reveals itself in rigid ability grouping (Cornwall, 2013; Marks, 2013). Working within this context means its relevance or usefulness cannot be undermined entirely but we do need to be aware of its dangers and limitations. This is explored more practically later in this chapter when the issue of differentiation is considered in greater depth.

Florian (2007) argues that the initial training of teachers should *demote* the Normative Model of difference whilst *promoting* the following alternative conceptualisations:

- An acknowledgement of difference as an essential, *normal*, everyday and typical characteristic of human development.
- A professional identity which embraces all learners and competencies for all learners.
- The incorporation of knowledge of human difference into a collaborative, problem-solving, solutions-finding context.

In this way, although student teachers will come across learners whose skills, competencies and learning styles are differently packaged, they will understand that it is their responsibility to shape their broader understanding of effective teaching and learning around individual differences. Florian (2007) argues that student teachers may come to see SEND as part of a spectrum of diversity rather than distinguishing these learners as separate and in need of specialist pedagogy of which they can never be availed. In developing and applying such alternative ways of thinking consider Task 3.2, and later an account of the *Spiral Spectrum Model of difference* which follows.

 Task 3.2 Constructing your personal model of diversity

If you were going to draw a picture representing how you see and respond to diversity in your class, what would this look like?

Student teachers tend to operate a Normative Model of difference in the earlier stages of their training but this becomes more sophisticated as they progress through their programme. Sometimes they will acknowledge that while their placement classes and schools might demand that they use ability grouping in quite a rigid way, they will apply more flexible ways of working and thinking. Below are three examples from third-year undergraduate students. You may wish to compare your drawing with theirs and consider how strongly they represent their philosophy about inclusion in their work.

Example 1: James and the jigsaw puzzle

James drew a jigsaw puzzle (see Figure 3.2). The pieces were different shapes and sizes but some of them shared the same pattern. James saw diversity in this way and he believed that it was his job to know about the similarities and the differences between all of the children in his class. For James, really *knowing the children* was key and assessment and interaction were the tools for this. In the end, it was his job to find ways of bringing all of the children together within one classroom community. This was why he had drawn all of the puzzle pieces fitting together into a whole picture. All of the puzzle pieces fitted together without losing any of their individuality or uniqueness. It was also noticeable that there was no distinct pattern for SEND as a separate or definable group. The approach to assessment and personalised provision explored in Part Two of this book adopts a similar conception of diversity and how to respond to it in the context of the mainstream classroom.

We're all different, but we are also all similar

Figure 3.2 Model of diversity (James)

Example 2: Lauren and the overlapping circles

Lauren acknowledges that children in her placement classes might be grouped by ability but also believes that it is important to recognise that these groupings are not always a true or full reflection of their developmental profile. With this in mind, she shapes her learning environment so that all the children can work and learn together. The circles and arrows in her picture show this interaction and overlapping. She has drawn a large circle around those representing groups within the class, and noted 'the circle around the model represents the teacher facilitating the learning and development of all children as well as learning from the children themselves'. A collaborative approach (with children learning together and teachers learning with children) is important to Lauren and part of her definition of inclusion.

Although children are grouped within ability groups – this is not a true reflection of children's abilities, as all children are individual and may differ in abilities regarding intelligence, compared to social or physical etc. Therefore, all children can work and learn together and from each other. So all children are included.

The circle around the model represents the teacher facilitating the learning and development of all children as well as learning from the children themselves.

Lauren

Figure 3.3 Model of diversity (Lauren)

Example 3: Sian and the pyramid of development

Sian has drawn individual spirals of different colours within a pyramid and written 'Individual needs in different areas within a pyramid of development'. This represents the developmental profile of one child who may be at different stages in different areas (such as social, emotional, mathematical, language, etc.). The spirals represent dynamic development (i.e. the child is moving forward and learning actively) and the pyramid represents this child's unique journey and their innate capacity to progress. Sian believes that it is important to have confidence in every child's ability to learn and make progress rather than focus on what they cannot do.

Figure 3.4 Model of diversity (Sian)

Introducing the Spiral Spectrum Model of difference

As a result of our research with teachers and student teachers (Trussler, 2011; Robinson, 2014), we have developed an alternative picture of diversity, the *Spiral Spectrum Model of difference*. When working with student teachers we present this as an alternative to the Normative Model. We do not wish to impose this or claim that it is the only and best way to picture diversity. Rather, we want student teachers to use the model when it is useful or view it as another option which has a number of positive possibilities. It offers a more inclusive conceptualisation of diversity as well as a tool for assessment and planning in the inclusive classroom.

Spiral Spectrum Model

We have used the Spiral Spectrum Model throughout this book. The spiral itself is intended to represent a continuum of development. The arrows have been used to depict where a particular individual is assessed to be, at a point in time, on the continuum of development for each characteristic.

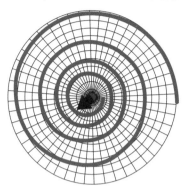
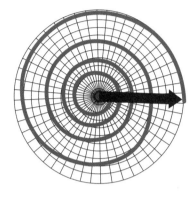

This would represent an individual at an early stage in their development

This would represent an individual at an advanced stage in their development

Figure 3.5   The Spiral Spectrum Model of difference

This model offers some conceptual advantages to inclusive practice and thinking as follows:

- It is more dynamic than normative or linear models and characterises development in a transformative way. Children are positioned within a dynamic developmental space that encourages us to see their capacity for forward movement.
- It represents the child holistically and captures the complex nature of their developmental profile. Hence, it counteracts a focus on deficits or on mono-dimensional conceptions of who a child is and what they are capable of. For example, rather than labelling a child as 'autistic' and assuming that this means holistic deficits, we can picture the unique developmental profile of that child and thereby secure more fitting, respectful responses.
- The spiral is value free with no representation of a 'norm'. Instead it conceptualises all development as normal. While a child with SEND may be at the earliest stages of development, this does not mean that those stages are not part of any other child's development or any teacher's understanding. Rather they are part of a natural and *acceptable* continuum of human development. In this way the spiral answers the challenges presented by Florian (2007) for ITE, because it encourages

a conception of diversity as a natural and inevitable characteristic of humanity.

- In not presenting a norm, the model detracts our focus from deficits and abnormalities.
- The spiral has all children *in* it and they are spatially close, rather than representing some features of diversity as marginal, outlying or other. In this way it can have a positive impact on professional identity since the stages of development it captures are not beyond the understanding or practice of ordinary classroom teachers. All children are *in it* and *ours*.

The second part of this book applies this model to the process of planning responses to diversity and SEND, and provides contextualised explanations for how it can be used to support you in developing more inclusive practices.

In summary, this section has critiqued the Normative Model of difference and presented alternatives to it. The aim is to help you identify and understand the impact of these models on our response to SEND. The following section takes this further in exploring the concept of differentiation and in offering new starting points for this important process.

Ways of thinking about difference and differentiation within the classroom

Alternative 1: The Normative Model as a starting point for differentiation

Many teachers may use the Normative Model as a shorthand way of conceptualising the diversity in a class and this can influence their approach to planning. For example, the nature of different classes may be visualised in the way shown in Figure 3.6.

The picture is different according to what proportions of children are attaining levels above, below, or in line with national expectations. Class 6B had less children working at significantly below age-related expectations and no children had been identified as having SEND. Class 3B had a smaller number of children working significantly above expected levels. Class 2R and 6B had a similar proportion of children working at expected levels but larger numbers of children of 'low ability' were in class 2R. You may have come across similar ways of thinking about diversity within a class but this way of thinking can lock teachers into particular starting points for differentiation that are not always promising for the purposes

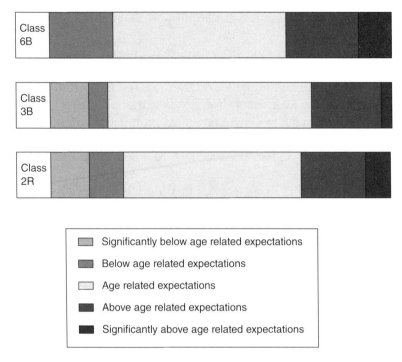

Figure 3.6   Range of 'abilities' in a class

of inclusion. It may reinforce particular ways of imagining or picturing diversity, as represented in Figure 3.7.

Figure 3.7   The 'Majority First' Model of differentiation

For example, it may lead teachers to consider the *majority first* in planning a learning experience. In this way, learning objectives and activities are designed to suit the majority. From there the objectives, task, resources and level of adult support would be adapted for those who were 'less able' or 'more able', resulting in different levels of task and children working in distinct ability groups. Arguably, this way of approaching planning for diversity dominates because this is the model encouraged by England's system of testing and accountability. English schools are judged on how many pupils reach or exceed expected levels of attainment. The school inspectorate expects to see such overt forms of differentiation as a sign of strategic intervention to secure progress (Ofsted, 2011). Incidentally, as noted in Chapter 1, the legislation in England also encourages teachers to associate provision for children with SENDs with doing something 'different and extra' as the definition of SEND in England also implies:

1. A child or young person has special educational needs if he or she has a learning difficulty or disability which calls for special educational provision to be made for him or her.

2. A child of compulsory school age or a young person has a learning difficulty or disability if he or she—

   i. has a significantly greater difficulty in learning than the majority of others of the same age, or
   ii. has a disability which prevents or hinders him or her from making use of facilities of a kind generally provided for others of the same age in mainstream schools or mainstream post-16 institutions. (Children and Families Bill, 2014, section 20)

With all of this in mind, the fact that teachers may adopt this way of thinking about differentiation is understandable and a reflection of the current policy context rather than their values. However, if you find yourself (for career or political reasons) having to adopt this or work within it, it will be necessary that you know about its limitations.

Corbett (2001) argues that ability grouping and individual interventions are perfectly acceptable as means of differentiating if they operate alongside other flexible, innovative and creative responses. Corbett created the term 'connective pedagogy' to describe her conception of inclusive practice. She notes that 'connective pedagogy' applies to all children including those with SENDs, and is concerned to demote the idea that children with SENDs need a different, extra or specialised approach. Corbett (2001) presents a Three-stage Model of differentiation and argues that where all three stages are at work, a school is more inclusive of all children including those with SENDs.

Differentiation operating at the shallowest level of inclusiveness (stage 1) will be limited to different levels of worksheets, tasks and interventions outside the class. Stage 2 will take responses to diversity to a deeper level. Varied pedagogies will be used to engage all learners and ensure accessibility in the context of whole class teaching. For example, a child with a visual impairment may be offered raised shapes to support learning during a lesson on 2D shapes, whilst these are also available to all children should they wish to use them. At this level, practitioners will make the effort to get everyone participating and children will be given opportunities to make their own choices and help each other. Teaching staff will be listening to the children's ideas and taking these forward. Stage 3 differentiation extends this into the whole school culture and ethos. Multiple pedagogies will be used within a culture that celebrates difference and there will be a concern to support individuals within a community where people work together to improve practice. Stage 3 differentiation is about attitudes and belief systems and is infused with the belief that all children can learn and that solutions can be found to secure the inclusion of all learners.

Hart et al. (2004) and Black-Hawkins and Florian (2011) are highly critical of an approach to differentiation that takes a majority first approach and which conceptualises responses to SEND as 'different and extra' for two key reasons. Firstly, this approach frames as 'different and extra' that which should be a natural, embedded part of inclusive practice. Secondly, it makes the minority an afterthought with the eventual consequence being an education system that continues to serve the status quo, leaving the minority as a group to be considered once the needs of the majority have been served.

There are some alternatives to the 'majority first' approach that have inspired more innovative and inclusive teaching. An explanation of these follows.

Alternative 2: Starting with everyone

Black-Hawkins and Florian (2011) argue that the question *'How can I design this learning experience for everyone including Johnny?'* tends to be underused to the detriment of inclusive practice. This is because it can trigger innovative and substantial changes that can benefit all children, including those who are most vulnerable.

You could ask this question as a starting point for planning differentiation in ways that may make learning more accessible for everyone. For example, Johnny might find it difficult to write fluently and if you were planning a science investigation you could ask 'What will make this learning experience and achievement possible for everyone including Johnny?'. This could lead you to choose a video recording or photographic recording over written forms. All children could access the learning and having 'everyone' in mind rather than 'the majority' means that overt forms of support (such as TA deployment or adapted worksheets) become unnecessary. It is not that such forms of overt differentiation are 'bad' but that they are sometimes unnecessary, and that it is important not to use this approach as the only one.

The cartoon in Figure 3.8 (Giangreco, 2007) is a metaphor for the value and logic of this approach. If the path clearer had asked 'What is the quickest way to get *everyone* in school?' the child in the wheelchair would not have been left waiting.

CLEARING A PATH
FOR PEOPLE WITH SPECIAL NEEDS
CLEARS THE PATH FOR EVERYONE!

Figure 3.8   Starting with everyone

Source: Reprinted with permission of the copyright holder, Michael F. Giangreco, © 2007

Another illustration of the value of the 'everyone' starting point is illustrated by the following scenario. Zobia was a second-year undergraduate student teacher and had been very proactive in meeting the needs of the class. One of the children in her class (Ben) seemed to find it very difficult to get started with his independent work. Although Zobia explained the independent task during the introduction, Ben avoided starting it and would wander about the classroom, sharpen his pencil and talk to others instead. To get him engaged, Zobia had put an individual reward system in place. Ben had an egg timer on his desk and if he started his work before it had run out he would get a sticker on his chart. This was working and it was pleasing to see that Zobia had given thought to this. However, when starting the task, children other than Ben were a little hesitant and were checking with each other what was needed. It is possible that if

Zobia had asked herself 'How can I make sure everyone understands the task?' and had built in some visual supports and reminders that may have resulted from this question, Ben would not have needed this individual intervention. In this way, using 'everyone' as a starting point can bring new ideas and ways forward and those approaches can benefit a wide number of children. Doing so can also save you time.

Approach 3: Starting with the individual

Another starting point is asking *'How can I plan this learning experience so that Johnny can succeed in the context of my whole class teaching?'*. Sometimes this can lead to changes of pedagogy that can have a positive impact on the learning of everyone, including Johnny. A second-year undergraduate student, Helen, found this to be the case. Johnny was a pupil in her placement class who had some difficulty staying attentive during a part of the lesson that we call 'carpet time' in England. Carpet time usually involves gathering all the children on the 'carpet' so that the teacher can lead learning in an interactive way. During this time there will be questions, discussions, explanations, modelled tasks, sharing of ideas and instructions. Johnny found it hard to attend to this so Helen developed a countdown system. When there were five minutes left to listen she would hold up a green card: she would then hold up a yellow card when there were two minutes left to listen and a red card when there was just one more minute. She found that this helped Johnny but that it also improved the attention and behaviour of many other children as well.

What is useful about this approach is that it triggers the design of new solutions and innovations. It can also reframe a child who is finding it difficult to learn as a solutions catalyst rather than a problem. Learning difficulties become triggers for innovations in our teaching so that all children can learn more effectively.

In summary of this section, there have been some alternative starting points for differentiation which can trigger new inclusive practices. No one model or starting point is perfect but the important thing is to use flexible and varied approaches in a creative way. Corbett's (2001) account of an inclusive pedagogy suggests that an inclusive connected pedagogy adopts the following character:

- It draws from many sources of ideas according to suitability.
- It is led by children rather than dominated by teachers – they have choices and options too.
- It draws on best practice from a wide range of sectors (including the special education sector).

- It involves stage 1, 2, 3 differentiation, but in relation to what works best for particular learners at particular times.
- It learns from the learners.
- It makes learning fun.
- It is not about convenience and routine. Always allocating a TA to a child with SEND or using different worksheets is not differentiation. Using identical group structures (including ability groups) is not differentiation.
- It has connections to sharing, supporting and encouraging.
- It recognises that no teacher or support staff should feel isolated and alone.
- It is based on support systems for children and teachers, which are flexible, non-judgemental and safe places in which creative solutions can be found without fear or bias.

Corbett's conception of inclusive pedagogy as connected pedagogy is important and useful as it emphasises the creative, problem-solving, collaborative, innovative nature of inclusive practice

 Reflection Point

Which starting points for differentiation have you seen used most commonly during your placements?

Which starting points for differentiation do you use most commonly?

How would you like to develop your approach to differentiation?

Summary

It has been argued that a positive professional identify for SEND is essential. If teachers recognise the relevance of their general skills to SEND they are more likely to engage in taking responsibility for learners who have this label. The chapter has also reviewed the strengths and weaknesses of various models of difference and differentiation, noting that normative models may lead to the domination of a 'majority first' approach which does not always give rise to the most inclusive practices. It has been argued that while the 'majority first' approach is helpful in

(Continued)

(Continued)

some circumstances, it is useful to have other starting points to hand when planning a learning experience, specifically considering the question 'What would help everyone to access this learning experience?' or 'What would help this child (who has the label of SEND) to access this learning experience?'. The aim of the chapter has been to support you in understanding and then operationalising a range of models so that you can select an approach that may result in the most inclusive outcomes for diverse learners.

Additional resources

The articles in this journal explore the impact of fixed ability thinking on teachers and children: www.wwwords.co.uk.ezproxy.derby.ac.uk/forum/content/pdfs/55/issue55_1.asp

This website explores alternatives to fixed ability thinking: http://learningwithoutlimits.educ.cam.ac.uk/

This resource examines (in a balanced way) the negative consequences that might arise from labelling children and not labelling them: www.tandfonline.com/doi/abs/10.1080/01411920802044446?journalCode=cber20

CHAPTER 4

INCLUSIVE CLASSROOM PRACTICE

Learning Objectives

After engaging with this chapter you will be able to:

- Explain how teachers' beliefs about SENDs impact upon the experience of learners in the classroom.
- Know about the pedagogic approaches which are likely to have a positive impact on the inclusion of learners with SENDs, considering how you could apply these findings to the design of the learning experiences you plan.
- Use criteria to evaluate the inclusiveness of your own (and others') classroom practice.
- Understand how to work effectively with learning support assistants so as to maximise inclusive outcomes for all learners.

Introduction

This chapter includes an analysis of contemporary research findings on effective inclusive practices and provides you with an opportunity to reflect on their relevance to your own work. Examples of inclusive classroom practice will be presented as a way of helping you to apply useful criteria for evaluating your own effectiveness. These illustrations will add life and colour to the exploration of what constitutes inclusive practice. Important and valuable contemporary research on the impact of learning support assistants on the social and academic inclusion of learners with SENDs will also be explored, with reference to implications for your own professional development as an inclusive practitioner.

The belief systems of inclusive teachers

Contemporary research provides evidence of the link between belief systems and inclusive practice. For example, in reporting on a long-term research project that took place in Canada (Supporting Effective Teaching) Jordan et al. (2009) found correlations between the models of SEND and ability that teachers operate, their teaching style, their overall effectiveness, and the impact of all of this on learners with SENDs.

Jordan et al. (2009) used an interview schedule which enabled the identification of perspectives. These two perspectives were the pathognomonic perspective (P) on SEND and the interventionist perspective (I) on SEND. The researchers were able to measure the extent to which individual teachers adopted these perspectives, with some teachers being strongly (P) or strongly (I) or somewhere in between.

A strong (P) score was attributed to those teachers who saw SEND as something that was *within* the learner. They attributed difficulties in learning to the child's impairment rather than to external factors. You may note that this perspective echoes the Functional Model described in Chapter 1. Using a range of methodological tools, the researchers were able to correlate a strong (P) score with the following:

- Belief in ability as something that was fixed and unmovable.
- Tendency to pass responsibility for learners with SENDs onto others and to use separate, segregated forms of support outside the classroom.
- Tendency not to collaborate with others in designing and delivering support for learners.
- Belief that they were not qualified to teach all learners.
- Use of formal teaching styles and approaches.
- Lower levels of engagement with pupils with SENDs.
- A tendency to use instructional interaction rather than deeper forms of interaction that might encourage higher order thinking.
- Less effective overall practice (e.g. in time management, classroom management).

A high (I) score was attributed to those teachers who saw SEND as something that was not fixed or within the child. These teachers attributed difficulties in learning to external factors such as teaching style or curriculum. Jordan et al. (2009) found correlations between a high (I) score and the following:

- Belief in ability as something that was not fixed but could change over time and was influenced by the effectiveness of teaching.
- Tendency to see learners with SENDs as their responsibility.
- Tendency to collaborate with others in designing and delivering support for learners.
- Belief that they were able to teach all learners including those with SENDs.
- Varied teaching styles including some emphasis on interactive learning and collaborative learning.
- High levels of engagement with pupils with SENDs.
- Tendency to use deeper levels of interaction to challenge learners' thinking, including those with SENDs.
- More effective overall practice (e.g. in time management, classroom management).
- Careful tracking of the progress of all learners.

Jordan et al. (2009) conclude that teachers' beliefs regarding their role and responsibility for working with students with SENDs influenced the extent to which they were willing and able to secure inclusion in their classrooms. Those teachers who accepted responsibility for all learners and adopted a Social Model of SEND were more likely to have a positive impact and to be more effective practitioners generally. They argue that inclusion might be dependent on a broader set of assumptions about ability, disability and how people learn. They also argue that effective inclusion may be analogous to effective teaching practices for all.

Other studies report similar findings. For example Nind et al. (2004) and Rix et al. (2006) surveyed existing international research evidence about the pedagogical approaches that were likely to impact positively on the social and educational inclusion of pupils with SENDs. They suggested that inclusion is more likely to happen where:

- teachers take responsibility for all learners;
- teaching styles promote higher order thinking and include interactions that provide a cognitive challenge to all learners;
- teaching styles invite learners to share their personal perspective, make their own connections, think for themselves, problem solve, engage in active learning and explore;
- learning environments encourage students to take ownership of their own learning and to work with others (pair work, peer support, group work);

- learning tasks are relevant, meaningful, and matched to learners' current experiences and levels of understanding;
- teachers have strong subject knowledge and are able to translate this into meaningful and accessible learning experiences.

There is much support for the value of social-constructivist approaches to inclusive practice. Social-constructivist approaches place social interaction at the centre of the picture and demand of teachers an ability to match their teaching to learners' current stages of development and experience. In this sense, social constructivism approaches teaching from the child out, starting with the child. From this perspective, teachers design scaffolds that support learners as they journey towards higher levels of skill or understanding. The following task will allow you to reflect on this idea at a deeper level.

Task 4.1   Identifying inclusive practice

Read the following case study on classroom practice and consider the following:

- To what extent is this classroom practice inclusive?
- To what extent are adults scaffolding this child's journey towards higher levels of skill and competence?

Case Study: Team work and scaffolding

Christopher (a child in the reception class) arrives at the 'creative table' where the task is to create a card dinosaur with moving parts. On the table there are pieces of white card, blobs of plasticine, laminated pictures of dinosaurs, information books, scissors, split pins, single-hole punchers, pencils and coloured pens.

Christopher is explaining to Claire (a third-year undergraduate student teacher) that he wants to do something different: 'I want to draw the picture out and around like this' (Christopher gestures with his hands to explain what he means) and after spending some time listening, Claire asks Geraldine (a TA) 'Can you help Christopher out a minute? He wants to draw round a template and I need to get back to work with the triangles group'.

(Continued)

(Continued)

Following Claire's request, Geraldine asks Christopher to come and sit with her and he does so immediately. He has a picture of a dinosaur with him and Geraldine asks, 'Which dinosaur have you got there?' and Christopher replies, 'It's a dinosaur!'. Geraldine says, 'It's a Tyrannosaurus Rex and he needs a body – can you draw him a body?'. Christopher smiles and draws a body on the card, and as he does so, he nods. Geraldine sounds impressed when she says, 'You see, you don't need a template!'.

It is quarter past two and Christopher is very focused on cutting out his dinosaur shapes. He continues cutting and is working without adult help with Geraldine at his side. Anna (the class teacher and mentor to the student teacher Claire) and Geraldine have a discussion about Christopher, and Geraldine gestures towards a file that she has with her (which contains assessment records). Geraldine and Anna praise Christopher together and affirm his effort and concentration.

Geraldine turns to Christopher and asks, 'How can we attach the straw to make these go together ... so we can make a hole in it and then what are we going to do?'. Christopher replies enthusiastically with 'Thread it!', and Geraldine says, 'You are going to thread it through – good boy!'. Geraldine speaks to Anna who is nearby and says, 'He knows what he's got to do Mrs Clark!', and Anna (the class teacher and mentor to Claire) says, 'Yes he does, well done Christopher!' Geraldine continues to support Christopher and he announces, 'I want to do some arms' to which Geraldine replies, 'You want to do some arms! Great, so go on then!'.

Your view of the practices illustrated above might differ from those of the practitioners who applied them since what is seen to be inclusive by one person may differ for another person. Additionally, it is important to know about the fuller and wider picture since the decisions that professionals make are often context specific and child specific. This is why inclusive practice cannot be reduced to a formula or recipe.

The practitioners in the case study identified highly inclusive practice within it because the student teacher (Claire), the TA (Geraldine) and the class teacher (Anna) had a collective understanding of Christopher's needs and collaborated to ensure that they took advantage of this opportunity to develop his creativity and independence. The team knew that Christopher preferred very 'safe' tasks and that he was reluctant to make decisions or take risks. Claire believed that this was why he had asked for a template: he wanted to be sure that it would look right, but she asked Geraldine to support him so that he could learn that he did not need to rely on a template and that his ideas and decisions were good ones. This collective knowledge and action was also evident in the interaction between Anna (class teacher) and Geraldine (TA) who made a particular point of praising his progress and noting its value.

Christopher had a statement of SEND and a diagnosis of Prader-Willi Syndrome, but the team was uncertain about the influence of this condition on his reluctance to take risks. For them, it was Christopher's individual needs that led their planning and response rather than his 'condition'. However, they did explain that this might not be the case in all contexts and forever, since more acknowledgement of his 'condition' might be necessary or helpful at other times.

It could be argued that this vignette does represent inclusive practice since it illustrates the whole team's collective efforts to match their responses to this child's needs.

Criteria for inclusive classroom practice

While it would be true to say that inclusive practice cannot be reduced to a recipe, it is sometimes useful to reflect on what it might look like in the classroom. The following task provides an opportunity for you to engage in this kind of reflection.

> ### Reflection Point
>
> When you are observing teaching and learning or teaching yourself, what would you identify as a sign of inclusive practice? For example, you might suggest that 'children engaged in their learning' or 'children having positive relationships with each other' would be signs of inclusive practice.
>
> Draw up your own personal criteria for identifying or evaluating the inclusiveness of classroom practice.

The criteria you create will reflect your own values and principles. The following is an illustration of the criteria designed by the staff and students working in the school represented by the classroom vignettes presented in this chapter. You may wish to consider how similar or different this is from your own criteria.

Table 4.1   Criteria for inclusive practices developed by students and staff in one partnership school

---

Routines
Classroom routines and the physical environment are designed to promote security in children, independence and equal opportunities

Personalised interventions
Individualised interventions occur and imply knowledge of children's individual needs (e.g. PLP targets, individual learning goals, emotional needs, interests)

Affirmation and positivity
Positive interaction, affirmation and rewards are used meaningfully (since they seek to promote progress, positive learning dispositions and positive relationships)

Warmth
Warmth, humour, openness and positive interactions between children and adults are features of the learning environment

Monitoring children's participation
Practitioners monitor who is involved and who is not and intervene to promote engagement, a sense of togetherness and equal access

Pupil independence
Pupil independence is enabled and promoted

Voice and ownership for children
Children are listened to and their choices respected. They can self-direct and operate creativity in the learning environment

Teamwork
The teaching team work together to enact the inclusive practices described in these categories

Communication and access
Accessible language and resources are used

Engaging activities
Activities are planned in a way that might appeal to children and their stages of development

Engagement and response
Children are engaged in learning and respond to opportunities to learn

Peer interaction
There is positive peer interaction between children

Parental involvement
The involvement of parents is evident

 Task 4.2   Identifying inclusive practice using criteria

Referring to the case study below, use the criteria presented in Table 4.1 to evaluate the inclusiveness of this practice.

Case Study: Dilemmas in inclusive practice

Christopher and Kirsty are in the role-play area. This has been set up to look like a dinosaur museum and there are trays of sand filled with bones, magnifying glasses, explorer costumes, a tent, toy dinosaurs and writing equipment. Kirsty has had an argument with another child and Christopher and Kirsty are talking about it. Christopher cuddles Kirsty and says, 'Why are you crying Kirsty?', and he touches her face in a loving way and seems to be speaking reassuring words to her that I can't quite hear, saying, '... and then you can ... and after that you can ... okay?'. He asks her what she is having for her dinner. She smiles and responds to his questions.

Another child is playing with a toy camera and Kirsty exclaims, 'I need that!'. The girl promptly gives it up. Kirsty uses the toy camera as a hair dryer and commences to play at drying Christopher's hair. They talk while this is happening. Anna (the class teacher) and Michelle (a TA) are watching Kirsty and Christopher and Anna asks, 'Is she drying your hair? Are you playing hairdressers?'. After a while, Michelle comes over and says, 'You are playing ever so nicely with Kirsty and you are playing nicely with Christopher.' The adult explains to Kirsty that Christopher has to go with her, 'He has had a nice time playing with you but now he has got to come with me', and Kirsty says 'Why?', and Michelle explains again. She draws Christopher away and Kirsty follows, seeming reluctant to give him up. Anna helps to separate Kirsty from Christopher and takes her to the role play area, engaging her in play. Later, Michelle explained to me that she had noticed the positive play between Kirsty and Christopher and had held off from interrupting them for as long as she could.

The professionals in this case study identified highly inclusive practice, since it showed that they had observed the positive interaction occurring between Christopher and Kirsty and had refrained from interrupting or ending the play because they were seeking to encourage more sustained peer interaction for these children. This could be evidence of their capacity to monitor participation, secure personalised interventions, enable voice and ownership for learners, and work as a team (the criteria shown in Table 4.1).

Reflecting on the classroom observation data and this particular instance, Anna (the class teacher) wrote:

From this data, I became aware of how sensitive the team is in responding to the needs of the children. I can see many instances where I am affirming and encouraging and where the design of the whole class environment is helping them to progress. This has given me a lot of confidence and this came at just the right time. The day after I had read the data, Christopher's mum requested a meeting with me and the head teacher because she felt that I was not including Christopher as fully as I should. We did reassure her but reading the data made me aware of something else too. Really, we should have left Christopher and Kirsty to play but because Michelle is his funded TA, she does individual work with him, and if that doesn't happen his mum might raise concerns about his entitlement. This is a bit of a tension really, but this data has confirmed that he is having a very inclusive experience.

The practitioners and Christopher's mother may be operating different definitions of inclusion, with the practitioners considering it in terms of inclusion within the class and Christopher's mother conceptualising it as individual support. This adds further weight to the claim that dilemmas and tensions are a constant and significant part of the context for student teachers and school staff alike. This has implications for you because you will gain from being able to justify your practice. Being clear about your values and principles can help with this and this is where criteria may be helpful. You may also need to make some compromises in managing the priorities of different stakeholders. The issue of managing tensions and dilemmas has also been explored in Chapters 2 and 3, given its significance to your work as an inclusive practitioner.

Working effectively with learning support staff

In preparing to teach inclusively, it will be important for you to develop strong team-working skills. The following section will explore the specific issue of how working collaboratively with learning support staff and TAs in your classroom can enhance positive inclusive outcomes.

A range of recent studies has confirmed the contribution that learning support staff can make to inclusion when particular forms of deployment and ways of working are in place.

For example, Alborz et al. (2009) report that when learning support staff are well supported and well trained, they can have a positive impact on the academic and social inclusion of learners, particularly in literacy. They can also reduce teachers' stress levels and enable them to work in depth with a wide range of learners and groups. When learning support assistants work sensitively with children (meaning that they interact in ways that foster independence and ownership rather than doing things for the child), they support achievement.

Blatchford et al. (2012) report similar findings about the positive impact of learning support assistants on the wellbeing and job satisfaction of teachers. They also report positive impact on the wellbeing and social participation of learners with SENDs. However, Blatchford et al. (2012) found that children with SENDs who had the support of a learning support assistant generally performed at an academically weaker level than those who did not. Since this was surprising, the researchers investigated the practices that were contributing to this outcome.

Blatchford et al. (2012) put forward the following suggestions about how to ensure that learning support assistants have a positive impact on the academic and social inclusion of learners with SENDs:

- Teachers and learning support assistants should spend time together talking about lessons and undertaking planning.
- TAs should not always work with 'less able' groups or children with special educational needs – teachers also need to do this in order to develop their knowledge of these children and develop the inclusiveness of their teaching more generally.
- The above helps because children no longer feel 'singled out' in getting additional support – rather it is something that is used at various times for everyone.
- Support should be used flexibly – the velcro model (that is, a TA being with a child all the time) is not as effective since it can be a barrier to independence and participation in the class community.
- TAs should encourage independent thinking and enable learners to be active in constructing their own knowledge. They should not do the thinking for them.
- The focus should be on the learning rather than the completion of a task. Teachers and TAs should be clear about what is to be learned from a task or activity and how that can be best promoted.

Similar insights arise in the wider research literature (Black-Hawkins et al., 2007; Villa and Thousand, 2005). This has implications for your own practice since you may need to consider how your approach to working with learning support assistants can be developed to enable positive inclusive outcomes.

In the wider literature there is powerful evidence supporting the view that collaborative working is a central feature of those schools that are most successfully inclusive (Corbett, 2001; Black-Hawkins et al., 2007; Sautner, 2008; Villa and Thousand, 2005). With this in mind it may be best to reject a professional identity for inclusive practice that depends on *lone perfectionism*. Instead, it may be more useful to see your professional future as one of continual learning, solution finding and team working.

Reflection Point

Having reflected on the issues raised in this chapter, list professional development targets that would support your journey towards being a more inclusive practitioner.

Summary

This chapter has outlined what is currently known about the belief systems and practices of inclusive teachers. It has also presented examples of inclusive classroom practice, providing opportunities for you to reflect on how you might identify and develop this. Throughout the chapter, the significance of social-constructivist approaches has been highlighted as has the importance of collaboration, communication and team work. Its purpose has been to support self-evaluation as you continue to develop as an inclusive practitioner.

Additional resources

The Canadian Education Association provides an account of the dominant stance on inclusive education as one of 'transformation' and is available at: www.cea-ace.ca/transforming-education

The statutory guidance supporting the 2001 Special Educational Needs and Disabilities Act contains descriptions of what inclusive schooling involves and what schools must do to achieve it. This is available at: http://webarchive. nationalarchives.gov.uk/20130401151715/https://www.education.gov.uk/ publications/eOrderingDownload/DfES-0774-2001.pdf

The Index for Inclusion (Booth and Ainscow, 2011) provides key indicators for inclusion including definitions of inclusion and criteria that might be used to evaluate the extent to which policy, practice and attitudes are supportive to inclusion within schools. This is available at: http://webarchive.nationalarchives.gov. uk/20130401151715/https://www.education.gov.uk/publications/eOrdering Download/DfES-0774-2001.pdf

The European Agency for Development in Special Needs Education (EADSNE) have developed a framework for developing key international indicators for participation in inclusive education. This is available at: www.european-agency. org/sites/default/files/participation-in-inclusive-education-a-framework-for-developing-indicators_Participation-in-Inclusive-Education.pdf

CHAPTER 5

THE 'SPECIAL PEDAGOGY' DEBATE

Learning Objectives

After engaging with this chapter you will be able to:

- Explain the debates surrounding special pedagogy and understand their relevance to your professional development.
- Understand three key concepts in the debate about special pedagogy: the general differences position, the unique differences position, and the continua of teaching approaches (Lewis and Norwich, 2005).
- Reflect on how you might manage the challenge of acknowledging impairment whilst resisting discriminatory practices or attitudes.
- Explain how Part Two of this book will help you to make inclusive responses to individual learners with SENDs in ways that promote equality and inclusion.

Introduction

In this chapter, the contemporary and significant debate about the existence of a 'special pedagogy' will be explored. This debate centres on whether or not learners who experience particular types of need (such as autism, moderate learning difficulties, Down's Syndrome) will require specialist pedagogies that are distinctive to that category (and distinctive from the pedagogies used for all learners). The debate also turns on the question of whether there are distinctive 'types' of learners who can be specifically and categorically identified. The chapter will also explore the importance of *acknowledging (and understanding) impairment* at the same time as *resisting the discriminatory attitudes and practices that might arise from a focus on impairment*. A range of key concepts will be explored, all of which are offered to support you in managing this tension. This chapter will also explain Part Two of this book where the focus will be on making responses to individual needs in ways that do not devalue learners or promote unhelpful ways of thinking about learning difficulties and disabilities.

Is there a special pedagogy for learners with SENDs?

The question of whether or not learners with SENDs require a special, specialist or distinctive teaching approach has been subject to vociferous debate.

As an example of that debate, Reid (2005) has reviewed the evidence base for specialist pedagogies as these relate to the category of learners to whom the label of 'dyslexia' is applied. He argues that it is inaccurate, inappropriate and unhelpful to believe that there is a prescription pedagogy that can be applied to all learners with ubiquitous positive effect for the following key reasons:

- While a range of common interrelated characteristics may contribute to dyslexia, it is also understood that there will be wide variations and differences in the extent to which individual children experience (or do not experience) these difficulties. Hence, seeking a 'dyslexia-pedagogy' is pointless since the group that the pedagogy is designed for cannot be served by a one-size-fits-all approach.
- Dyslexia is best understood through a complex causal framework where behavioural, cognitive, neurological, environmental and cultural factors come into play. Hence it is unlikely that any one approach would be universally appropriate since dyslexia is experienced in learner-specific and context-specific ways.
- The research evidence cannot confirm the existence of a specialised pedagogy. For example, various approaches to teaching phonics have been evaluated and there is no single approach that seems to be the panacea. Further, the approaches to phonics training suggested for learners with the label of 'dyslexia' are not necessarily distinct from good practice for all children, including those who have reading difficulties but are not considered 'dyslexic.'

- The research evidence does confirm that learners who experience dyslexia benefit from the same approaches as other learners, particularly when these approaches are varied, multi-modal, cross-curricular, multisensory, delivered through high-quality teaching, holistic (with recognition of the social and emotional dimension), and carefully tuned to the needs of individual children. It is not that these are different in character, it is that they may be learned and taught in more intensive and deliberate ways (for example, at a different pace, with more opportunities for practice and more careful structuring).

Reid (2011) argues that we should view the teaching of dyslexic children from the perspective of *specialised knowledge of the learner* incorporated with the application of a *wide range of teaching principles and learning approaches*. Hence, being prepared to teach learners with dyslexia requires expertise about the learner combined with a broad pedagogic repertoire that can applied in flexible and focused ways to bring about the best outcomes for groups and individuals.

Elliot and Grigorenko (2014) give further support to this position, noting that dyslexia as a category may not be helping us to understand or respond to the diverse range of literacy difficulties present in our classrooms. It can also lead to an unjust system of resourcing since those who are struggling to acquire literacy but are not labelled with dyslexia are vulnerable to neglect from the education system. It must be acknowledged though that this suggestion is strongly resisted on the grounds that dyslexic learners need special attention and special support in order to experience equal opportunities. Whether they need a clearly distinctive teaching approach is another question however and one that is subject to continuing controversy.

Having explored 'dyslexia' it would be useful to consider another 'type' of difficulty so as to capture the complexity of the debate – autistic spectrum disorder (ASD).

Arguably, there is more support for ASD as a distinguishable category than there is for 'dyslexia'. Jordan (2005) notes that while it is important *not* to consider learners who experience ASD as entirely distinct from all other children nor ignore the uniqueness of each individual, it is helpful to acknowledge the distinct and stable group of difficulties that are characteristic of learning and development in ASD. These comprise difficulty with social communication (using communication skills to receive and transmit spoken and non-spoken language), difficulty with social interaction (using social cues, empathy and interpretation to read other people and respond appropriately) and restricted, repetitive patterns of behaviour or interest. ASD also involves sensory sensitivities or difficulties. It is interesting to note that the American Psychiatric Association (APA) have amended their diagnostic criteria by combining social communication with interaction (APA, 2013). The APA have also removed the distinction between autism and Asperger's Syndrome given a lack of evidence about the difference between high functioning autism and the latter. Arguably, this demonstrates how the stability and fixedness of 'conditions' and 'categories' may actually be illusory, and why you might need to be tentative in drawing conclusions about learners on the basis of the label they have been given.

Jordan (2005) argues that in the case of ASD there are specific forms of pedagogy attributable for this group, noting that learners with ASD may need a curriculum approach that compensates for difficulties (to enable access) and also provides therapeutic approaches (to remediate difficulties such as anxiety or sensory issues). Teachers who work with learners with ASD need to understand the complex cognitive and psychological difficulties experienced by this group. In the case of ASD, effective education may involve different and additional approaches rather than just more of the same.

Jordan and Jones (2012) emphasise that a genuinely inclusive approach to ASD would also acknowledge that the impact of ASD is dependent on an interrelated complex factors. Hence, the extent to which the *impairment* ASD becomes *disabling* depends at least in part on the environment. Jordan (2005) also notes that inclusive practitioners would recognise the unique variability of all learners and so resist making assumptions about how one child or another experiences ASD. Jordan (2005) calls for an education system that might better respond to human individuality and variation through being more flexible and fluid in its approach to teaching and a curriculum design for *all*. For example, we know that many learners who experience ASD need more time to process information but we also know that many learners without ASD also need this time. If the education system could adopt more flexible ways to accommodate variability in processing speeds and styles, all children (including those with ASD) could benefit.

Reid (2011) and Jordan and Jones (2012) argue that whilst it is important to *acknowledge and understand impairment*, it is also essential that we do not allow *impairment* to overwhelm our perception of the learner as a unique and complex individual who (like all learners) has things in common with others and things distinct from them. Consequently, we are charged with making decisions about which teaching approaches would be most fitting with the needs of the learner, within a particular context at a particular time for a particular purpose. There is no magic bullet or prescription pedagogy that can applied. The pursuit of a magic formula or of a perfect, everlasting solution is futile, and it is more productive to seek ways forward *in context* through calling on a wide range of pedagogic skills and insights about how children learn and develop. Part Two of this book is designed to support you in developing your skills in this area, with particular reference to assessing individual learners and responding to them in the context of the inclusive classroom.

In summary, the evidence supporting the existence of a special pedagogy for learners with particular types of needs is ambiguous and uncertain. However, knowledge and understanding of impairment can support informed, inclusive practice (for *some* learners in *some* schools among *some* teachers) when these are viewed as one part of a complex picture. Chapters 2 and 3 provided further support in how to conceptualise impairment so as to secure inclusive teaching and learning. The next section describes other concepts that may support your understanding of effective pedagogy for SENDs.

Concepts related to special and inclusive pedagogy

Lewis and Norwich (2005) provide a conceptual basis for considering the extent to which teaching approaches for SENDs are specialist or not. Before these are examined, the following task will help you to understand your own conceptual position on this so as to support your engagement with the theoretical frameworks that follow.

 Task 5.1   Considering your conceptual position on special and inclusive pedagogy

Imagine that you had a child (called Katy) with the label of 'Down's Syndrome' in your class.

Put the following statements in order from top priority to bottom priority:

- A: To be prepared to teach Katy effectively, practitioners need to have in-depth knowledge of Down's Syndrome.
- B: To be prepared to teach Katy effectively, practitioners need to have in-depth knowledge of Katy.
- C: To be prepared to teach Katy effectively, practitioners need to have in-depth knowledge of how to assess and teach all children effectively.

In our own research (Robinson, 2014) all of the student teachers and practitioners we worked with (including those in special schools) believed that 'B' (expert knowledge of the child) was the priority, noting that it was not possible to operationalise 'B' without 'C' (expertise in assessment, teaching and learning) since one depended on the other. For example, if a teacher is not skilled at assessment, their ability to develop in-depth knowledge of Katie (B) would be limited. Further, if a teacher does not have a broad range of teaching skills and approaches to draw on, their ability to put what they know from 'B' into practice in 'C' would also be limited. This tends to echo the arguments put forward in Chapter 3 since it has been demonstrated that those teachers who are effective at including learners with SENDs are also effective teachers of all children (Jordan et al., 2009). The relevance of teachers' more general skills and knowledge base to inclusive practice should not be underemphasised or undervalued. Everything you are learning on your initial training programme or as a beginning or experienced teacher is relevant to being an inclusive practitioner.

Returning to the authors' research (Robinson, 2014), student teachers and practitioners took a more ambivalent view on the relevance of 'A' (expertise in Down's Syndrome) since they believed that while accessing this knowledge base might be important (for the sake of their own preparation), the extent to which this *could* and *should* be applied to Katy was dependent on the context since a generic description of Down's Syndrome may or may not relate to Katy's individual profile as a learner. They would not want the label to become oppressive in limiting their perception of her potential or overshadowing her uniqueness.

Student teachers who are in an earlier stage of their programme tend to place more certain value on 'A' (expert knowledge of Down's Syndrome). This may be because lay people (who are not yet members of the profession of teaching or do not have much experience of SEND) take up the more traditional view that there is a medically diagnosed, qualitatively different type of person who needs a special form of education. This may arise from the historical and policy context (as is explained in Chapter 2), given that for much of the past century learners with disabilities were certified by medics and sent to separate, specialist institutions. For the sake of your professional development as an inclusive practitioner, you need to leave such crude conceptions of diversity behind and embrace a more nuanced and sophisticated perspective. This has been explored and applied in Chapter 3 with particular reference to models of difference and differentiation.

The general differences position and the unique differences position

Lewis and Norwich (2005) offer a conceptual basis for the position you may have adopted in Task 5.1. If 'C' (knowledge of the category of learners to which Katy belongs) was prioritised as a basis for preparation, this would reflect the *general differences position* where differences are accommodated within distinct groups or sub-groups. When adopting this position, the belief that the needs of a sub-group can be met by pedagogies that are specific to that group is regarded as valid. Hence there is a concern to seek category-specific pedagogies and group profiles as a starting point for planning a response. Knowledge of individual needs and knowledge of effective practice for all learners would still be important but positioned a little further in the background.

Arguably, the general differences position may be adopted by agencies and professionals who are promoting specialist or expert identities in a particular field or type of difficulty. In part it would support their status, and in some cases rightly so. However, the general differences position (and its inherent emphasis on impairment and category specific pedagogies) can be justified for *some* learners in *some* categories (such as ASD), but it is unlikely to be a universally valid basis for making an inclusive response given the contextual complexities of individual children and classrooms.

The *unique differences position* (Lewis and Norwich, 2005) takes a contrasting view.

This is a position that assumes that while all learners are different they are also, in a general human sense, the same. Differences between individuals are accommodated within this position, not in specific categories, groups and sub-groups. From this perspective, categories (like dyslexia and ASD) are not as relevant since pedagogic choices are informed only by common and individual needs. The standpoint that 'good teaching is good teaching for all' is attributable to this position and it is believed that the generally effective teacher has the skills and expertise necessary to understand all children's needs. The unique differences position is one that is often adopted by those who promote inclusion and there has been a trend towards it in policy (see Chapter 2).

In evaluating the relative validity of these two positions, Lewis and Norwich (2005) report that there is a lack of evidence to support SEND-specific pedagogies (and hence the general differences position), but that where there is evidence this supports a unique differences position.

In summary, while it is not helpful to discard what is known and understood about particular types of impairment, the unique differences position may be more fitting with inclusion. It also gains more support from the research evidence. In applying what is known and understood about impairments, it is necessary to be cautious and acknowledge the unique variability of individual learners, teachers, classrooms and schools. In this sense, a falsely tidy and fixed conception about what groups or sub-groups of learners are (in terms of their characteristics) and need (in terms of pedagogic response) is misleading and may trigger exclusive practices and attitudes.

 Reflection Point

Reflect back on Task 5.1. On the basis of your initial response, which conceptual position did you adopt (general differences or unique differences position)? Having read about the potential limitations and possibilities of both, has your position changed?

Continua of pedagogic strategies for diverse learners

Lewis and Norwich (2005) apply a framework for thinking differently about inclusive pedagogy for diverse learners, including those with special educational needs.

The *continua of pedagogic strategies* emphasises that teaching approaches for SEND are not necessarily *qualitatively* different but are *quantitatively* different, namely that they draw on the same basic principles but are more intensive, involving for example more frequent practice in smaller steps across a range of modalities. Figure 5.1 illustrates this.

Usual adaptions	Intensive adaptions
– Pupil-led – Larger steps and longer-term goals – Few examples – Self-evaluation and monitoring	– Explicit and teacher-led – Over learning and much practice towards mastery – Many and varied, multi-sensory approaches – Repetition – Frequent – Explicit, frequent teacher monitoring

Figure 5.1 Special pedagogy as a quantitative rather than qualitative difference

This model of pedagogy *may* offer more helpful ways of thinking about the relationship between SEND and pedagogic design for the following reasons:

1. It offers a more fluid and flexible conception of pedagogy for SEND and for all. For example, the more intensive approach may be as applicable to a learner who is exceptionally able but has a specific difficulty in one area (such as spelling) as it would be to a learner who has more global learning difficulties.
2. It prevents unhelpful splitting of pedagogic approaches. For example, a strategy traditionally used for learners with the label of ASD (such as using sensory preferences as a way of securing engagement) may be as beneficial to learners who do not have the label of ASD. There is potential value in borrowing approaches usually applied to one group and adapting these for another.
3. It illustrates the idea that pedagogy for SEND is more quantitatively different than it is qualitatively different. Hence it may support mainstream teachers in developing a positive professional identity for inclusive practice since they can see how their usual practices are not entirely distinctive from those that they could use to good effect with learners who have the label of SEND.
4. It may enable alternative interpretations since strategies that might on the face of it appear very alien and distinctive, may in principle be the same as those more commonly used.

Summary

This chapter has explored the debate about whether there is a 'special pedaogy' for learners with SEND or not. As illustrated, this question has prompted wide debate. Conceptually, practitioners may take a general differences position (in which they regard the group or category of difficulty as a useful and reliable starting point for planning pedagogic responses) or a unique differences position (in which the unique learning profile of learners is seen as the most reliable starting point for planning). It has been argued that while the general differences position may be useful in some cases and some contexts, teachers need to be cautious about placing their trust in the 'label' as a reliable basis for planning a pedagogic response. This has implications for your professional development, since in preparing to be inclusive you will need to be sceptical about training

(Continued)

(Continued)

sessions that may provide you with neat categories of SEND and category-specific strategies that offer a quick fix. The diverse learners you will meet in the future will confound such simplistic and superficial conceptions of human difference. In some ways, it is their job not to conform to text-book descriptions of what they should be. In some ways also, it is your job not to conform to traditional ways of thinking about difference and responding to it.

Part Two of this book places more emphasis on the processes of assessment and planning for individual learners. You will remember from Chapter 3 that an alternative model of difference underpins the approach taken in Part Two. This model is the *Spiral Spectrum Model of difference* and it offers a more dynamic approach to conceptualising difference so that the colourful and complex uniqueness of learners is embraced in ways that might support inclusive outcomes.

Chapter 7 will explain how and why the Spiral Spectrum Model is being used as a basis for personalised planning and what it might offer you as a means of developing your practice.

Additional resources

www.drgavinreid.com/
Gavin Reid has constructed a very useful reference which presents a range of papers and resources related to inclusive teaching approaches for dyslexia.

Black-Hawkins, K. and Florian, L. (2011) Exploring inclusive pedagogy, *British Educational Research Journal*, 37: 813–28. doi: 10.1080/01411926.2010.501096.
In this article, the authors present a case against 'special pedagogy' on the grounds that it diminishes inclusive outcomes for all.

www.diffability.com.au/
This resource publicises additional and specific teaching programmes available for learners identified as autistic. You may wish to evaluate whether these programmes are *quantitatively* or *qualitatively* different from education for social skills for children who do not have autism.

PART TWO

CHAPTER 6

STRENGTHENING THE 'WHOLE CHILD' APPROACH THROUGH THE SPIRAL SPECTRUM MODEL

Learning Objectives

After engaging with this chapter you will be able to:

- Explain how theoretical knowledge can underpin good practice in meeting the needs of a range of children within the 'average' classroom.
- Consider how labelling children in order to gain funding can lead to a barrier for the effective teaching of children as individuals.
- Understand how operating a particular model of inclusion and special educational needs can lead to preconceptions of what pedagogies to use in class, particularly that there might be something specialist in teaching children with SEND.
- Plan for an individual approach to child profiling to support the most effective organisation of learning and teaching.

Introduction

The stance taken in this book has been that the more you understand about how inclusion works and about the challenges faced by teachers in decision making for children with SEND, the more you will be ready to respond effectively to your unique and varied pupils.

In this chapter, the value of a 'Whole Child' Approach is explored and the practicalities of treating every child as an individual in a challenging classroom are examined. Throughout the chapter there will be opportunities to reflect on your model of inclusion, as well as how this is possible to realise when there are competing pressures of meeting an inclusion ideal and labelling children in order to get funding. A possible framework for meeting these challenges will be presented in the *Spiral Spectrum Model of difference* and its practical application in the *spectrum 'dashboard'*. These are tools that can help identify individual needs and support the configuration of groups within the classroom to most effectively teach children for all areas of development, not just the cognitive. Hence, a concern to understand inclusive education within a holistic framework is demonstrated.

How does understanding theory help a teacher?

From the outset of this book, the idea that our belief systems impact on our capacity (and our willingness) to be inclusive has been asserted. Throughout Part One we explored a range of theories on what inclusion is and how it might be enhanced. We also looked at the impact of particular perceptions of SEND on outcomes for learners. An opportunity to reflect more on this is provided in the following task, in direct relation to an individual learner, Emma.

Task 6.1   Understanding Emma

Emma is 6. She is lively and happy. But Emma is constantly sent out of the class for non-compliance. What could we understand about Emma that would help us appreciate why she is non-compliant?

- The teacher could be pitching the lessons incorrectly, providing work that is either too hard or too easy. Either way, Emma would not be engaged by the work set so becomes non-compliant.
- Emma could have challenges working with other children. Perhaps she is the youngest in her family and used to getting her own way or having things done for her. Because of this, when she is asked to work as an equal in a group she finds this too challenging and becomes non-compliant.
- Emma may lack attention at home. She feels secure and safe at school and knows that if she misbehaves she will get attention. She does not like to make her teacher cross, but when she gets sent out of class the behaviour manager really listens to her and she likes that.

(Continued)

(Continued)

- Emma could have a learning delay, so she is not being naughty but reaches the limits of her concentration very easily, and then becomes non-compliant.
- Emma may have a condition such as ADHD where she needs to learn what is good behaviour as well as what is non-compliant behaviour. She lacks the social awareness to pick up on cues for compliance like the other children, but she could learn with patience and repetition.

 Reflection Point

Consider one of the children in your class who struggles to comply. Think about the reasons presented above: what could be a reason to explain why this child finds compliance difficult? Children are not 'just naughty', there is a rationale for all children's behaviour. If you and your colleagues are prepared to take the time to learn why a child behaves the way they do, you can support them in managing this.

Let us take a look at each of the reasons above and consider what we could do to support Emma in each of those circumstances:

- The teacher could be pitching the lessons incorrectly, providing work that is either too hard or too easy. Either way, Emma would not be engaged by the work set so becomes non-compliant.

Emma could be using non-compliance as a strategy for the teacher not to recognise that she is particularly able or is unable to do the work set. It may be surprising that children may not want you to know they are particularly able, but this does happen. Sometimes very able children do not want to be viewed as different. Sometimes they find it challenging to try an open-ended task because they do not want to risk making a mistake – rather than make an error, they would rather not do the task at all, so become non-compliant. For teachers it is hard to measure progression along an area of development without evidence, so this needs to be found in different ways. Verbal questioning, group tasks, non-written tasks can all yield clues to a child's capability that simply sitting them in front of a written exercise may not. You need to be a detective, open minded to whatever you may discover without preconceptions.

- Emma could have challenges working with other children. Perhaps she is the youngest in her family and used to getting her own way or having things done for her. Because of this, when she is asked to work as an equal in a group she finds this too challenging and becomes non-compliant.

Emma needs a role within the group in order to feel valued and responsible. The children in her group are not going to be patient with her if she expects them to do her tasks too. Therefore, the teacher needs to carefully configure a group that has mature children and those who are able to take on compatible roles. Vygotsky expounded the theory of the zone of proximal development where children learn from those with slightly more knowledge than themselves – a 'more able other' (Pass, 2004). This can apply to learning about behaviour as well as cognitive learning. So Emma would have role models within the group, who she knows are praised for their good behaviour; these role models would help her transition from immature behaviour to that expected within the classroom.

- Emma may lack attention at home. She feels secure and safe at school and knows that if she misbehaves she will get attention. She does not like to make her teacher cross, but when she gets sent out of class the behaviour manager really listens to her and she likes that.

This is a tricky cycle to break – as a teacher you become frustrated and you apply the school's sanction policy that results in Emma being removed from the classroom after a series of warnings. It is difficult to utilise different behaviour strategies from those for the other children when Emma does not appear to have a particular individual need beyond attention seeking. What is key here is to find opportunities for Emma to receive attention for good actions within the class. Giving her a responsibility within the classroom – taking the register to the office, watering the plants, giving out books – can provide a distraction from early low-level disturbance. Behaviour charts can also be a visual opportunity for Emma to demonstrate her good behaviour and being rewarded for it. As she begins to enjoy praise for her successful behaviour in the class, she will settle and comply within the normal parameters of the classroom.

- Emma could have a learning delay, so she is not being naughty but reaches the limits of her concentration very easily, and then becomes non-compliant.

In these circumstances the teacher would need to work out if Emma can cope with a whole day in her current class. Perhaps she would do better with time in a younger class so that her social and emotional needs are met as well as her cognitive ones. If a one-to-one assistant were available, Emma could have a curriculum designed for her needs which could be taught in small time chunks so she does not become overwhelmed. Frequent breaks would allow her the chance to play and then re-engage. Emma could also take part in whole class lessons that would be more practical in nature so she does not become isolated from her peer group. She should receive many rewards for her compliance rather than focusing on sanctions for when she cannot comply.

- Emma may have a condition such as ADHD where she needs to learn what is good behaviour as well as what is non-compliant behaviour. She lacks the social awareness to pick up on cues for compliance like the other children, but she could learn with patience and repetition.

Children with ADHD are generally able to learn behaviours, but teachers need to understand that these behaviours will be learned and not instinctual or intuitive. A range of visual cues, rewards, repetition of expected behaviours, patience and acceptance that behaviour management strategies may have to be applied differently, can lead to success.

So Emma seemed quite a simple case initially – she was non-compliant. But an awareness of the different potential answers and the theory that underpins these enabled the teacher to find a solution that would support Emma's chances of learning to her potential and de-escalate her behaviour. However, she is just one member of the class. As a teacher, you will need to find the stories for all your children so that they fulfil their potential.

The relevance of child development to inclusive practice

If you have an awareness of the trajectory of development for children in a range of areas (social, emotional, physical, communication, cognitive) then you can plan the next steps for children. In addition you can understand the strategies to use if a child is delayed in relation to others in the class. Children do not develop consistently and along 'typical' milestones – you can have an understanding of the way in which children generally progress, but equally importantly you need to have an open mind as regards individuality in development, and possess the tools to create a learning environment that accommodates and nurtures children wherever they are in their individual development journey. You can plan teaching that enables a child who is further developed in one area or challenged in another, and you can balance the social and emotional needs of children with the physical or cognitive.

Many initial teacher education courses do not cover child development any more due to time constraints or because the training relies on schools providing the academic input, which is why this text has broken down the use of the Spiral Spectrum Model along the lines of child development areas. Development is complex, but understanding children as individuals is imperative to effective personalised teaching and learning.

The impact of labelling on teacher perceptions

In Chapters 1 and 2 we examined the models of SEND and inclusion. Simply put, the models fell into two broad categories: functional (associated with a Medical Model) or transactional (associated with a Social Model). Medical models relate to a conception of the child as being able or disabled; social models relate to an understanding of social, political or environmental factors impacting on the ability of a child. As reported in Chapter 1, our own research (Robinson, 2014; Trussler, 2011) identified the problem that teachers may appear to adopt a Social Model of SEN when discussing inclusion, but a medical one when talking about individual children because this relates to the way we rely on categorising children in order to entitle them to mainstream provision. Teachers are conscious that for some elements of their provision children need to have a label, even if in the classroom they do not. If they were involved in the statement-making process for example, the teacher may well have to apply the labelling to the child ('dyspraxic', etc.) rather than the setting ('inclusive', 'lacking resourcing') which still firmly places the child's 'problem' at the root of provision. It's hard as a beginning teacher (and even an experienced teacher) to appreciate the nuances involved here. The challenges set by this contradiction were explored in Chapters 2 and 3.

On entering a classroom for the first time, teachers may introduce children to you as 'being dyslexic' or 'this is the SEN group'. This can immediately set up a barrier for you to teaching the children. They have become a different group, a group that may need special planning or teaching. The following case study activity will help you consider what the impact of this may be.

Task 6.2   Considering the impact of labels

Read the following case study and reflect on the impact of the Social and Medical models on outcomes for Joe.

Joe's mother takes him to the doctor because he does not seem to be developing in the same way as other children. The doctor looks for symptoms of an illness or condition. The doctor thinks that if he identifies symptoms he will be able to find cures and therefore help to make Joe better. The doctor decides that Joe may have autistic spectrum disorder and refers him to a psychologist. Joe's mother is given a leaflet about the symptoms of autism and the challenges this presents for education. Joe's mother then goes to his school. She meets his teacher and asks how he is getting on in class.

- What would she expect to hear if the teacher followed a Medical Model of disability?
- How would the teacher describe Joe in the classroom if she followed a Social Model?

Let us consider the different sub-models within each tradition and how these might impact on how Joe is described: put a tick in the box that best categorises the statement to the left. These sub-models are explained in Chapter 1.

We are not suggesting that one approach is right and another wrong, rather let us consider the difference the approaches might make to teaching and hence to the outcomes for Joe.

Medical Model: in this model the difficulties lie within the child – in our case study we compared this to a doctor looking for symptoms. As a teacher, you might consider that having a list of symptoms for a condition would help with teaching. For example, if you know that children with a visual impairment would need things in large print, then that helps you plan for lessons.

What are the advantages and disadvantages of this approach?

Advantages: you can create a guide for each condition that enables teachers to plan ahead for the children in their class. There is then consistency in the approaches taken to support children.

Disadvantages: Every child is different; two children with the same condition can have very different needs, abilities and require different approaches. A list of common characteristics does not help every individual.

Table 6.1   Medical and Social Models

The teacher said:	Medical			Social		
	Medical/Deficit	Tragedy/Charity	Support/Services	Social	Capability	Socio-political
I feel so sorry for Joe, he doesn't have many friends because of his condition						
I change the groups around so Joe can work with other children						
Joe needs a different curriculum and a one-to-one support assistant or I cannot teach him						
There is clearly something wrong with Joe, autism sounds right						
Joe is very good at maths and his reading age is good						
It would help us get funding to have Joe diagnosed with autism, so we can help him						
I find using a visual timetable and clear communication useful for Joe and the other children in the class						
I find it frustrating that we have to label Joe 'autistic' – it helps for funding, but I don't use the additional support to segregate Joe, but to help integration						

Social Model: in this model there is an understanding that the environment impacts on children's learning. It presents a view that politically children may be disabled by the educational system due to the requirement for labelling and funding categories. It also acknowledges that, although children may have a medical, psychological or physiological condition, it is not the condition that disables a child but the way we view it.

What are the advantages and disadvantages of this approach?

Advantages: When teachers consider the whole environment, rather than individual children, this can result in effective educational provision for a range of children. It leads to an understanding that children do not require specialist teaching, just consideration of their abilities and needs.

Disadvantages: You now have to consider the needs of each child, rather than being able to group children according to their SEND. You need to be flexible in your teaching approaches, being prepared to respond to children's reactions to curriculum and pedagogy.

The arguments above lead us to consider a discourse of disability and SEND that will clearly influence teacher and student teacher practice and school identity. This discourse includes notions about their own roles and circumstances: whether they have to obtain resources or support for a child and whether the environment in which they practise is accommodating and supportive for children with SENDs to reach their potential, fully included in the learning environment.

As a beginning teacher, it is very difficult to try approaches to children's grouping and teaching that are different from that of the usual class teacher. However, it is worth evaluating the approaches taken by the class teacher and talking with them about why they have chosen the strategies they have. You can gain an appreciation of how they view SEND and which model they are employing, and then consider what the outcome is of this perspective. Are all the children well included? Are they treated as individuals? Are they viewed as having capabilities or inabilities?

The complexity of these issues may impact on student teachers as they engage in teaching children with special needs, particularly with children whose teachers or SENCOs may have expressed the view that the appropriate resources or support are not in place. Despite this, though, it is worth remembering that they are all children. Simply stated – if you see children as having abilities you are going to view them as children who *can*; if you see children as having disabilities you will view them as children who *cannot*. This sounds trite, but is a test you can apply to how you perceive children with SEND. If you start with a 'can do', you are going to be prepared to change the environment, behaviour strategies, pedagogy, the assessment model and the configuration of groups, to ensure that all children have a fair chance to access the curriculum. If you start with a 'cannot', you will be planning for the 'typical' child in the class and will view the others outside of this band as different, difficult and requiring something of you that may not be easy to provide (this idea is explored in further theoretical detail in Chapter 5).

So how do you teach the range of children in a mainstream class if teaching SEND is not a specialist activity?

It is not a surprise that teachers view teaching children with SEND as a specialist activity. There are special schools, children have special educational needs – this sounds as though there would be a special approach required. There are also particular resources or approaches that certain children will need – for example, large print, signing, wheelchairs, etc. which are related to their needs, but very often the teaching strategies that work for children with special educational needs prove to be good teaching strategies for all children.

Children's areas of development operate along a spectrum. Children in the average class will have developed at various stages along this spectrum. But by suggesting that teaching all children is possible for all teachers and just requires a few strategies and identification of needs along a continuum, there is a danger that children with special needs will not have all their needs met as teachers are not necessarily able to recognise and meet medical, social, emotional or behavioural challenges. We have to recognise the differences between children in order to enable them to reach their potential – and perhaps the push for inclusion has failed to acknowledge that 'same' (as in setting or aspiration) does not necessarily make things equal for children.

A conclusion that teachers within all settings must use a continuum of strategies to meet the learning needs of children, may be a relief to those who are concerned that there is some mystery to teaching children with special educational needs. However, it does have significant implications for initial teacher education as it requires beginning teachers to gain confidence in recognising when a child is requiring them to move along the continuum and provide intense support and when general provision is sufficient. It also requires of them a recognition of what 'intense support' looks like for a child with a particular need at a particular time. This is a challenge, but it will be necessary to find ways to build your confidence and competence in this area with the background knowledge to judge an appropriate approach for a particular individual. You will be presented with different perceptions of teachers with whom you work and for some this idea of continua of development requiring continua of teaching strategies will be difficult to accept.

Reflection Point

So how do you develop your perceptions? How can you evaluate your own perceptions and their effect on your teaching?

Firstly, consider the complexity of schools: every teacher has to not only learn to participate in the teaching aspect of schools but also get to grips with the reification of events through self-evaluation and observations and reports of others. You will encounter perceptions of every event in school: one teacher's interesting class is another teacher's nightmare; one interprets the inclusion policy as a misguided approach, another as an ideal to aspire to. Everyone who works within a school brings not only their previous life experiences and perceptions, but also their way of interpreting what they see, hear and experience in school. So as you reflect on your own perceptions, consider how far these are congruent with those around you and how far you are reflecting your life experiences, beliefs and values in the way you set up and teach your class.

It takes experience to be able to confidently find your own persona and identity as a teacher. These may not emerge immediately and your self-efficacy as a teacher will come as you develop confidence and competence, and you are able to reflect on the experiences you are receiving and find an approach that suits you and works for you. So how does that self-identity emerge? How will you know that you are developing into the sort of teacher you need to be?

Obviously you will be assessed against competence standards (in England, the *Teachers' Standards*: DfE, 2011), but in terms of teaching children with SEND, as you have seen, there are various approaches which a teacher can take that would be considered appropriate. These may include an ability to communicate with colleagues about their role, not just about children in the class, and to provide them with frameworks for evaluating their own thoughts and recognising from which model or perception they were functioning.

How might this work?

You can evaluate your own perceptions and values, placed within a theoretical framework related to the classification of special educational need, and how this is going to impact on your teaching identity and approach.

- I believe that people should be …
- I believe this because …

 Reflection Point

How have you developed your political, social and moral values? Generally these would have come from family and personal experience. Responding to the following cues and questions will support you in clarifying your own philosophy.

How would you describe your values?

Think about how these relate to your desire to be a teacher and what sort of teacher you want to be. This will become your philosophy of education – what children should be getting from education and your role in enabling this.

- Education is …
- An effective teacher is one who …
- A successful education is one that …

Now think about how this relates to inclusion: think about the models of SEND we examined earlier – how does your view of education fit with these models? Look at the models – which ones feel right to you?

- How does all of this fit with what you have seen in school?
- How are you going to let your model of SEND influence you as a teacher?

You might have had to face the fact that the legislation of a certain time and practice are not congruent with your value system; you may have wanted to adapt curricula and strategies to meet your own agenda for inclusive practice; but fundamentally you are going to have to rationalise intellectually this potential dilemma of difference. As well as considering the impact of your values in relation to inclusion, there is also value in considering the impact on children's self-perception.

So now reflect on how your values, attitudes to SEND and perception of yourself as a teacher will impact on children:

- If you were a child with SEND – in what sort of environment would you like to learn?
- How would you like a teacher to perceive you – as a learner, as an individual?
- Does this impact on any of your answers above?

Introducing the spiral spectrum dashboard as a tool for personalised planning

For all children in a class teachers are aiming for an awareness of individual needs so they can plan ways to ensure that all of those children reach their potential. The Spiral Spectrum Model outlined in Chapter 3 enables a teacher to profile each child across the six areas of development – ignoring labels and preconceptions – so that comparisons can be made and planning can be undertaken for learning across the curriculum. The spiral does not specify ages or 'typical' development milestones, instead it is a comparative tool to enable teachers to reflect on children's abilities and group these appropriately for the range of curricular areas. So, for example, a group of children may be towards the centre of the spiral for emotional development and therefore will require a particular approach to personal, social, health education (PSHE). However, only one of those children may have a labelled special need such as autism because the others have different reasons for being where they are on the spectrum (e.g. family separation, bereavement, illness). They will all require the same sensitivity of approach regardless of why they happen to be in similar positions within the spiral. Chapter 3 provided an explanation of the theoretical basis for this model and how it developed from our research (Robinson, 2014; Trussler, 2011).

Below is the *spiral spectrum 'dashboard'* that can be created for each child based on their respective position along the spiral in relation to their peers. This may seem like a lot of work when you are also assessing reading skills, maths ability, etc., but it can help you remain impartial and focus on the range of abilities for each child so that you can plan for all areas of development and not just cognitive. This can help you plan activities for each lesson that will recognise a child's ability to work in a group for example, or to have the physical dexterity to cut out intricate patterns for an art lesson. We tend to group children according to their cognitive development, but some activities rely as much on the other elements of development to be successful. Grouping children in ways that support their holistic development can lead to a more secure learning environment and, potentially, more successful outcomes.

As you read the dashboard, the spiral represents the full spectrum of development within a particular class or year group. You will notice that it does not have ages attached and nor does it present learning as a linear process. The arrows pinpoint where a child is in relation to their peers: the closer to the centre of the spiral the earlier the stage of development in comparison, the further out the later the development. You may think this is just presenting the usual labels in other ways, but by eradicating labels this enables teachers to access very visually the range of development across a class in each area as well as an individual profile of a child. When we group according to cognitive development alone, we ignore a child's other facets. We also tend

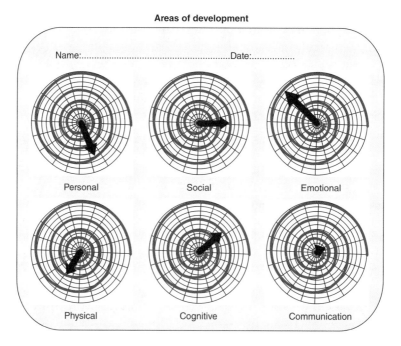

Figure 6.1   Dashboard example

to make assumptions, such as the 'better able' (using typical labelling) a child the more mature they are – whereas in fact they may have earlier emotional, personal and social development. Children who we currently label as 'SEN' may in fact have later development, in physical development for example.

 Task 6.4   Using the spiral spectrum dashboard as a tool for planning an inclusive response

Below is Penny's dashboard. How would you describe her current stages of development?

- Personal.
- Social.
- Emotional.
- Physical.
- Cognitive.
- Communication skills.

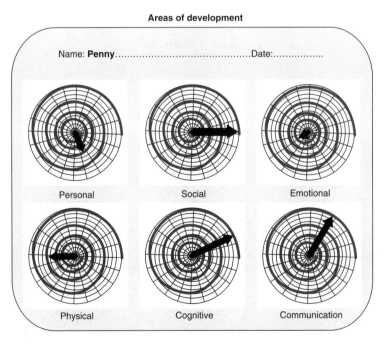

Figure 6.2   Penny's dashboard

How would knowing this impact on your teaching?

Key factors that would influence your decision making regarding lesson planning include:

- Penny is able to work well with others;
- she is aware of how her mood can influence others, so she tries to be friendly;
- Penny finds the work challenging but because she is socially aware, she tries her best;
- she finds explaining her thoughts very difficult and, at times, can become upset because other children can get frustrated with this.

Now have a look at these three dashboards – which child would you sit next to Penny and why?

- Do you choose the child with the same personal, social and emotional profile?
- Do you choose the child with the same cognitive profile?
- Does the physical profile make a difference?
- I would choose Neema – why do you think that might be?
- Have a look at Neema's profile and assess why I might make that choice.

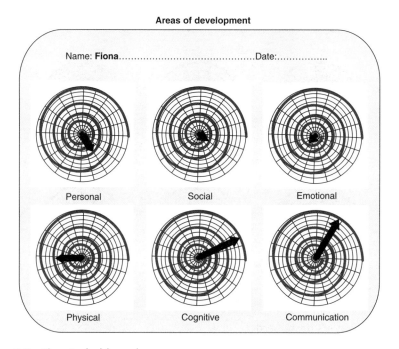

Figure 6.3   Fiona's dashboard

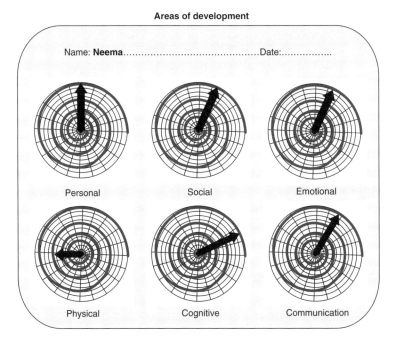

Figure 6.4   Neema's dashboard

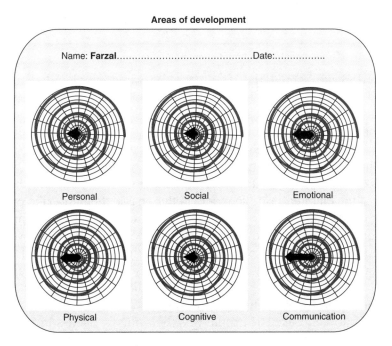

Figure 6.5   Farzal's dashboard

Consider the advantages of sitting her next to a child who is at a later stage of development in terms of cognition. That could also be Fiona, so why would I choose Neema rather than Fiona? If Neema or Fiona were to act in the role of peer teacher for Penny, who would be most likely to be empathetic with Penny's difficulty with communication? The value of the dashboards is that you can consider the widest range of abilities within the children when planning for classroom organisation, curriculum input and assessment. This is the essence of educating the whole person. It is also fundamental to truly inclusive education as you will be considering the widest profile of the children, with no labels and preconceived expectations.

One of the significant values of the spiral spectrum dashboards is that they also indicate when children's profiles change. This then informs your teaching approach. This is also what was meant earlier in the chapter by teaching across the spectrum and intensifying support where it is required rather than having a specialist pedagogy.

Task 6.5   Reflecting on progression using the spiral spectrum dashboard

Take a look at Zeek's and Blake's spiral spectrum dashboards and decide which personalised approaches they might lead you to take.

Zeek and Blake started the year with the same profile. Both children required support related to emotional development when they were engaged in academic work. So, when introducing new topics, the children would need support to try new skills and lots of praise when they did enjoy success. Because they were not as fully developed cognitively as their peers, they needed work that was differentiated for their respective level. Therefore rather than just focusing on academic work, valuing the other aspects of the children's profile would better enable them to make progress.

Looking at their profiles in May it looks like Blake made no progress. However, these spirals are comparative so he will have made progress but did not close the gap with his peers. Group work, preferably mixed ability, would work well with Blake as he has social awareness and self-esteem, so would not be intimidated by children who were achieving academically and would enjoy contributing.

So what about Zeek? His profile was the same as Blake's in September but changed dramatically by May. Why might this be? The two aspects

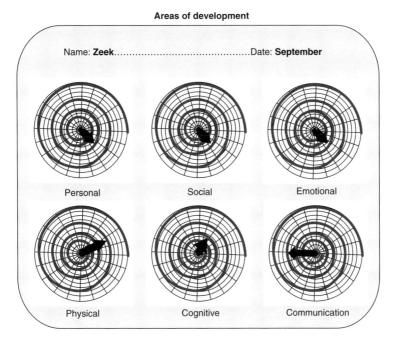

Figure 6.6   Zeek's dashboard in September

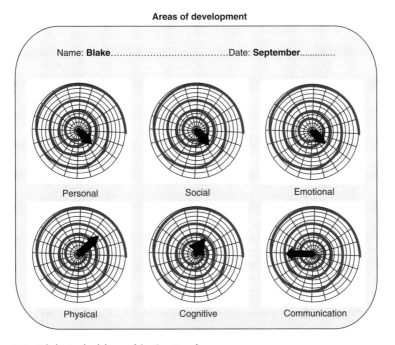

Figure 6.7   Blake's dashboard in September

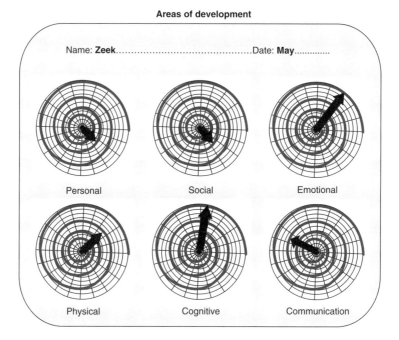

Figure 6.8 Zeek's dashboard in May

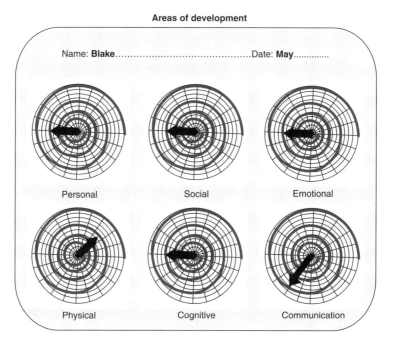

Figure 6.9 Blake's dashboard in May

of development that have made a significant progress were emotional and cognitive. What could be the reason for this? Perhaps Zeek had experienced an emotional setback the previous year which had resulted in him not making the academic progress of which he was capable. Perhaps he had been unwell for a period of time. The input they both required in September was the same, namely support with emotional and social development together with the differentiation required to build on academic skills. If it had been assumed that Zeek's cognitive profile in September was his potential, this could have led to low expectations and hence less progress.

Both children required at the beginning of the year the same teaching approaches. As the year progressed changes would have been made, reflecting the developing profiles. This describes the continua of approaches from earlier in the chapter. If children are defined solely by one area of development, or by the profile they first present to the teacher, then they risk missing out on reaching their potential. As teachers we can best serve our children by being alert to changes as these occur across all areas of development. This results in teaching that is focused on the child and not just on delivering the next topic; it is flexible and utilises ranges of groups, resources, approaches and strategies.

Summary

In this chapter we have explored values and attitudes to the models of SEND explored in Chapter 2 that affect the resultant teaching strategies. We developed an understanding of the Spiral Spectrum Model and its use in classroom practice by using the concept of a spiral spectrum dashboard. This included looking at similar spirals and how these can change over the course of a year's teaching.

As an outcome of the chapter it has been suggested that the use of spirals to profile children can suggest effective teaching strategies that address more than one area of development and can enable children to reach their potential.

Additional resources

http://webarchive.nationalarchives.gov.uk/20060213205517/standards.dfes.gov.uk/personalisedlearning/
The personalised learning agenda website from the original 2005 document.

www.gov.uk/children-with-special-educational-needs
The Department for Education (DfE) guidelines on special educational needs.

Berk, L.E. (2003) *Child Development* (6th edn.) Boston, MA: Allyn and Bacon.
In this text, the author outlines a detailed perspective on child development and places what is considered 'typical' development within a theoretical and sociological context.

CHAPTER 7

PERSONAL, SOCIAL AND EMOTIONAL DEVELOPMENT

Learning Objectives

After engaging with this chapter you will be able to:

- Define personal, social and emotional development (PSED).
- Use the Spiral Spectrum Model as a way of making an inclusive response to diversity in the area of PSED.
- Apply the Spiral Spectrum Model to case studies of individual learners within the context of an inclusive classroom.
- Consider how adapting whole class teaching and the whole class learning environment might secure inclusion for learners at diverse developmental stages in PSED.

Introduction: who am I?

When I describe myself I tend to use words about my physical features: I have blue eyes, I am short, I have blonde hair ... Are you the same? How often would you use a description of your self-esteem, your self-confidence or your self-image?

Can self-esteem, self-confidence or a positive self-image be taught? Should it be the remit of primary schools? This chapter will explore these issues and how integrating the facilitation of a child's PSED is imperative in the holistic and inclusive education of children. It will apply the Spiral Spectrum Model to personalised planning for personal and social development. This chapter is based on the premise that as

educators we are hoping that children become effective, knowledge-able learners who can explain their approach to learning, who have a strong belief in their own abilities and who have the confidence to take risks in learning. They can only do this if they have been guided through the stages of PSED appropriate for their individual circumstances.

So, does having personal, social and emotional together mean that they are the same thing? Why do we tend to put them together and how do we meet the needs of children in them individually and combined?

Definitions: personal, social and emotional development

Personal development relates to our unique combination of attitudes, values and characteristics that make up our personality. As we grow older we gain a better understanding of our personality and we also gain a perception of our 'self' – an identity. Our perception will not necessar-ily match that which other people have of us and this is part of the development that schools can support.

Social development is the way in which we learn how to interact with others. In their very early days, babies learn who to trust through consist-ent meeting of their physical and emotional needs which helps them form attachments to family and carers. As children grow older socialisa-tion broadens to include friends, schools and communities. These are challenging stages to go through for a child as they bring together many other personalities and children with many other experiences prior to nursery or Reception.

Emotional development describes how a child gains an understanding of their emotions, how to describe how they feel and an awareness of how their feelings impact on others. With effective emotional development sup-port, children can develop high self-esteem because they will know that they can generate positive emotions in others and that they have self worth.

So while it is obvious that each element has a particular meaning, it should also be apparent that these work in combination. However, defi-nitions only describe what a concept means, they do not describe the individuality of each area in terms of how these impact on each child. So what can influence how children develop in personal, social and emo-tional elements? These will be important things to consider when you are planning an inclusive, personalised response.

Family circumstances and PSED

Early attachments are key to security in PSED. Theorists such as Bowlby and Erikson emphasise the need for consistency in early attachments for future security and emotional stability. If babies experience many changes of carer, or a lack of response to their crying, they learn that their needs will not necessarily be met – they grow insecure, perhaps more needy, and therefore making more efforts to be heard; perhaps distant and untrusting of relationships. This very early lack of support can be overcome by future nurturing, but would impact on children's early education and absorption into early schooling.

As children grow up, families grow and change together and experience many life-changing episodes. The impact of experiences such as ill health, death, divorce, relocation and the transition between Key Stages or schools will be unique to each individual. For some these will cause temporary change emotionally and not impact on long-term personal and social development. For others small changes to routine can have an effect, so major life events can cause long-term problems which may then require specialist help to overcome.

Poverty is still one of the biggest determinants of educational success. In terms of personal development, long-term unemployment or a lack of educational success in parents can negatively impact on how a child views their potential and their self-concept as a learner. Endemic messages can be hard for children to overcome and can also be reinforced by a lack of resources within the home and by parents' inability to bridge the gap.

Children's awareness of any special educational need or disability will impact on their self-perception, regardless of whether the nature of the special need would impact itself. For example, a child in a wheelchair may well develop a strong, positive outlook with secure management of their emotions. However, that self-concept will include their perception of themselves as disabled and how they can engage in their learning environment and with others. Their disability in itself does not determine the child's path of PSED, but it will affect it. Children on the autistic spectrum, however, will have a different development pattern from what might be considered typical in PSED. Social communication, relationships and flexibility of thought are three of the four aspects of development – with sensory being the fourth – which are different in children with ASD compared to children with more typical development patterns. As such, they will require specific support and teaching to follow the same developmental path and would, most likely, not reach adulthood with what one might consider to be typical emotional responses or reactions to social situations. Other conditions such as attention deficit hyperactivity disorder (ADHD), dyspraxia, Down's Syndrome, foetal alcohol syndrome, will all affect PSED to some extent, and there will be a lack of understanding in children of how they can progress unless specific input is provided.

So what can be considered to be 'typical' development?

Often theorists will suggest that aspects of child development follow a 'typical' pattern, with approximate ages being attached to each stage of development. The word 'typical' is problematic for an inclusive practitioner since it is value loaded. It is more relevant to consider development as a flow from birth onwards, so that whilst milestones are not important the characteristics of development are helpful in planning next steps for children.

In terms of personal development, key aspects for teachers are that personal development relates to children being able to locate themselves within a culture, gender and community. By school age, children will have generally understood that they are a boy or a girl and they are learning their family background. As they grow older the focus moves on to developing self-esteem and identity as an individual. This can be an uncomfortable journey as children compare themselves to others and learn about personality, character and physical image.

In social development the focus is on awareness of others and by school age children generally will have had experience of different social groups. Children may have experienced a fear of strangers and new circumstances and these can be enhanced or lessened by attending pre-school environments. As a child proceeds through school they are expected to learn to adapt to group situations and effectively function with other children in order to learn. This can be a challenging experience as it is expected that children will feel confident speaking in front of others – accommodating other children's needs and desires and adapting themselves to learning collaboratively.

For emotional development key development points include an ability to manage emotions and not responding instinctively as they did pre-school.

Children are expected to develop a basic empathy with others by the time they enter the last years of primary school. In addition they are expected to 'read' others' emotions and respond appropriately to these.

The Spiral Spectrum Model and PSED

As we have seen before, life events can impact on development – so if a child experiences ill health, bereavement, parental separation, their progress may be stalled or even reversed. Especially in aspects of child development such as PSED, the impact can be significant and potentially long term. The Spiral Spectrum Model presents development as a series of strands spiralling outwards without age-related targets and it normalises all differences, working on relative differences rather than milestones. Children can slide along the spiral and the various elements of child development can be positioned at different points of the spiral without this being considered abnormal. For teachers, it then becomes a case of identifying where each child is on the spectrum and working from this starting point to identify next steps. This demands a personalised approach to learning and teaching as no one child will have exactly the same profile.

Task 7.1   Using spiral spectrum dashboards for PSED

Look at the two spirals below for PSED. Identify which child has autistic spectrum disorder.

Did you choose Spiral 1? This is probably because you have heard that children with autistic spectrum disorder have difficulties with social and emotional interaction, so their development is comparatively delayed. You chose very logically. But if I told you that the child in Spiral 1 was the youngest of four children and found leaving his mother very difficult in the morning, was still speaking in very short phrases and was so upset in school that he had not made friends, and also that it was September in a Reception class and child 1 was apparently very able but was not integrating well, you could see why Spiral 1 was the logical choice for him and not the child with autism. The difference, however,

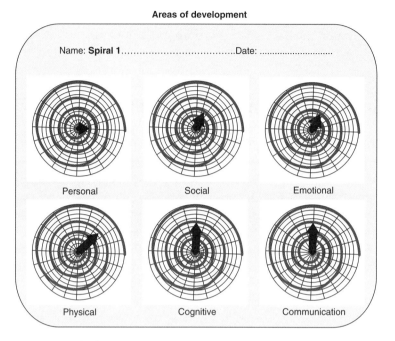

Figure 7.1 PSED Spiral 1

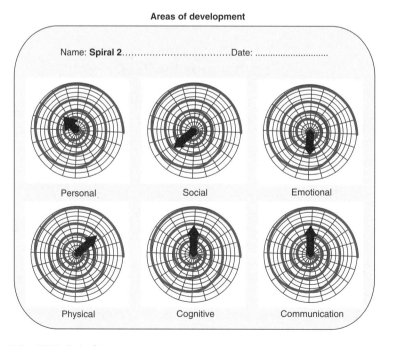

Figure 7.2 PSED Spiral 2

is that child 1's position on the spiral could change rapidly as soon as the teachers and TAs had worked with him on his attachment issues and he had found his feet in the classroom, whereas child 2's spiral may not move or change significantly.

The teacher in this case used the spirals as relative measures – she was not worried about age-related milestones but comparing the children in her class so that she could group children appropriately and find relevant activities and interventions for them to make progress. In this way, she found that she stopped using terms such as 'high ability' and 'low ability' and started to measure progress in more explicit ways. This meant that she was able to describe each child in more detail – she was also able to measure the impact of certain changes more appropriately. She did set children for different learning sessions, not just against their cognitive development but dependent upon the learning objectives: she also set for physical development or social development. For example, one of the children in her class was very boisterous, but when the teacher completed the spiral for this child, she found that the child was unable to explain her emotions, so when she was trying to make friends she became physical and children did not respond well. With additional help related to her social development and her emotional literacy, the child overcame these difficulties and became more emotionally and socially aware with high self-esteem.

   ## Task 7.2   Reflection on a case study

For the child described below, try to identify the potential impact on the PSED of each element of this child's story. Complete Table 7.1, considering implications for learning and teaching:

Tom is 6 years-old. He lives with his mum and three sisters. His mum does not work because his little sisters are only a few months and 2 years-old, and his other sister is 5 and in the year below him at school. Tom's mum has experienced some difficulty financially and he often comes to school without breakfast. He is on free school meals. As the oldest child in the family, Tom often has to look after his sisters when his mum goes out, sometimes at night as well as during the day. He is a very caring child and usually plays with younger children at school. With his peers he can be intimidated by their play and tends to stutter when he feels pressured or exposed. Tom is sensitive and at times can be very tired and lethargic.

Table 7.1 Tom's story

Aspects from the story	How it may impact on PSED	Implications for learning	Implications for teaching
Tom lives with his mum and three sisters	May impact on Tom's self-image – potentially as 'the man of the house'	Tom may want to engage in kinaesthetic learning or physical play	The teacher needs to observe Tom's learning style and facilitate this, but also offer him alternative learning experiences to provide him with a range of skills and aptitudes

1. *Each element of the case study could be interpreted in different ways.* It is only through careful observation that the teacher can measure what these circumstances have meant to Tom. We all react to situations differently.
2. *Mum does not have much money so this can result in the family having to prioritise basic needs over luxuries.* As a teacher, you could help the family access resources like a range of reading books through a trip to the library as a class, which would excite Tom and enable him to explore reading outside school for no additional cost. The impact of poverty on achievement is well documented, so a school's use of homework clubs, breakfast clubs and access to information and communications technology (ICT) within school can help families overcome any deficit in home resources.
3. *He looks after his sisters.* This is a situation that impacts on his social and emotional development, but it can also be considered as neglect, so would need to be reported to the school's safeguarding officer. It might, however, provide Tom with high self-esteem as a good older brother, and this could be used within the classroom with Tom supporting a child who may struggle in a particular subject area. Tom then becomes what Vygotsky calls the 'more able other' in the learning situation, which may help with his sensitivity in the learning environment and raise his confidence with his peers.
4. *Teachers do not always have the answers, but at least if they have carried out careful observations, they have the questions.* For Tom's stutter, for example, the teacher may want support from a speech therapist to find strategies to help him overcome this tendency.

Understanding what theorists such as Vygotsky (Pass, 2004) say about how a child develops and learns can help teachers plan the next steps for children. Tables 7.2 and 7.3 outline some key theorists who have relevant theories for PSED.

So what is effective pedagogy for PSED?

There are several steps to effective pedagogy for children in order to meet their PSED needs:

1. *Observation* – identify the children's abilities individually: gather information about the children's home life and their position in the family; formulate a picture of the child.

Table 7.2 PSED theorists

Theorist	Theory related to PSED	Relationship to pedagogy
John Bowlby 1907–1990	Attachment Theory: secure attachments are formed where babies have consistent care from adults, they do not necessarily need to be parents, but do need to be familiar and provide nurture, not just basic needs.	Where attachment has developed healthily, children are able to leave family with few problems when they start school. Where a child is 'looked after' or receives erratic care from adults who are unable to provide their basic needs, the transition to school can be very challenging.
Erik Erikson 1902–1994	For Erikson, each developmental stage was characterised by a crisis that had to be faced by the child. If successfully overcome then personality is resilient and strong. For the youngest children the stage is trust/mistrust. At this stage children who have attachment disorder, and do not have the trust that their caregiver will return or provide consistent care, will experience further difficulties with trust.	What do you think would be the impact on a child who does not trust when they come into school? The child may lack consistent routines and rules. They may be clingy or detached. How would a teacher in the Early Years handle this?
Jerome Bruner (1915–) Lev Vygotsky (1896–1934)	Socio-cultural Development: Learning happens in a social context. For children to progress they need to be able to interact with adults and more able children. Vygotsky introduced the notion of zone of proximal development which is the next stage of understanding for a child that they get through with a 'more able other'. Bruner developed this with the idea of scaffolding where the child is enabled by carefully planned steps to make progress.	Although these strategies are elements of cognitive development, how would a child with low social and emotional development cope with these ways of working? If a child finds interaction with adults and other children difficult, how are they going to find social constructivist learning? How would you as a teacher provide the support for children in this position?

(Continued)

Table 7.2   (Continued)

Theorist	Theory related to PSED	Relationship to pedagogy
Albert Bandura (1925–)	Social Learning Theory: In Bandura's 'Bobo doll' experiments he discovered that children would copy adults' violent behaviour if there were no apparent consequences. This indicated that children were taking social cues from adults, but also that their moral awareness was manipulated by the situation.	How would this impact on learning in the classroom? It indicates the strength of the impact of effective adult interaction with children and modelling. How could you utilise this knowledge of negative influence to create a positive one?

2. *Create the class spirals* – the Spiral Spectrum Model is designed to be comparative, so each spiral is developed in comparison with others; once you have a picture of each child, you will be able to plot their position on the spiral for each strand – one for personal, one for social and one for emotional development, compared with their peers. The aim is not to place relative values on each child or on their stage of development as compared to a class 'norm', but to gain a picture of the developmental diversity in your class so that you can adapt your universal and personalised provision in ways that are responsive to this developmental diversity.

3. *Lesson planning* – when planning for each lesson examine the personal, social and emotional implications of that lesson to decide on learning objectives based not only on the subject but also on how they will be delivered. This might impact on group work – so perhaps rather than always grouping according to perceived ability, you might want to support a child's social development by pairing children where a more able child could act in a teaching role and they work together to problem solve. This could raise the self-esteem of both children as one is learning how to teach, thereby reinforcing their self-image as a learner/teacher, while for the other their self-efficacy is enhanced because they have taken on a more challenging task than usual and been able to achieve it.

4. *Teaching* – acute awareness of children's PSED enables you to be sensitive to children's needs as you teach. You can challenge those who are ready to speak out in whole class situations, you can use non-verbal methods for those who are not. You could support children's social development with the use of talking partners and thinking trios. You could also encourage emotional development through appropriate

but frequent praise. Stimulating, challenging, engaging teaching reduces the need for behaviour management because children are focused on the learning – this then helps build an image of the class as a community, and most especially a learning community. For all children this is a positive development and one where they will feel safe making mistakes and taking risks in learning. Once a child can do this, they have reached high levels of PSED.

5. *Assessment* – we are used to assessing children's cognitive development, but as we have seen in this chapter, the holistic development of children is vital to their perception of themselves as learners and to the way in which they will approach learning. So alongside the assessment of learning objectives related to subject knowledge, you will also need to assess how children's personal, social and emotional objectives are being met. Formative assessment – assessment for learning – should occur continually in the classroom. This can be a very easy way to reinforce children's perceptions of themselves as learners and can positively affect their self-esteem and self-perception – children need to know how to learn as well as what to learn. Effective target setting that includes personal, social and emotional goals form the basis of children understanding themselves as well as understanding the curriculum. Children can then self-evaluate across a whole range of measures – this also acts as emotional literacy, being able to describe themselves as social beings as well as learners.

6. *Evaluate* – to complete the planning and teaching cycle there is evaluation. Evaluation includes looking at children's progress as well as our teaching. Reflection on how children are progressing along the spirals needs to be part of a regular review of progress. It can influence how we teach and how we interact with children. Evaluation is not looking for the negative, but reflecting on what has worked, what teaching strategies have been effective, and building on those to ensure that progress for all children continues.

Task 7.3   Observing practice

During your placement experience (or in any lesson where you are not the class teacher), carry out an observation similar to the following. Observe a learning session from start to finish and note down the frequency of the following types of interactions (you could use tallying so that you can note down quickly):

(Continued)

(Continued)

Table 7.3 Observation sheet

Observation	Tally
How many times the teacher speaks	
How many children speak during whole class situation	
How often the teacher comments positively on behaviour	
How often the teacher comments negatively on behaviour	
How often the teacher praises a child for an aspect of PSED*	
How often the children comment on themselves as learners	
Can you think of anything else that might indicate how far the teacher is accommodating PSED in their teaching?	

* this could include comments on being helpful to another child; on being confident enough to speak; on being able to say how they feel about their learning …

What was the balance of teacher talk to child talk? If the teacher talked more, did this prevent the children from taking ownership of their learning? What was the potential impact on their social development?

How often did the teacher comment positively on behaviour compared to negatively? What was the impact of positive comments compared to negative ones? How would this impact on the children's social and emotional development? If the children hear negative comments about their behaviour, how do these impact on their self-concept?

What strategies were used to facilitate assessment for learning and, therefore, for enabling the children to understand better how they learn?

Now repeat the exercise, but this time video yourself teaching a session. Does your teaching change when you are conscious of the things you noticed in the other class teacher's lesson?

PSED and special educational needs

A central question to ask (and one that was explored in Chapter 5 in relation to the special pedagogy debate) is if there are children at different ends of the spectrum, does this mean that those children need specialist teaching?

The Spiral Spectrum Model is designed to demonstrate that children follow a journey in development, so though children with special educational needs may be at different stages on the spectrum, they may not require 'specialist' teaching. There may be specialist elements to working with children with SEND (for example, creating Braille materials for a child with visual impairment, or using Makaton or the picture exchange communication system (PECS) with children who have communication challenges), but in order to support the inclusion of children with SEND teachers need to exploit the strategies that they use usually, and if they are not 'usual', they may have to make them figure as such. The difference is that the teacher knows the abilities of all the children, so also knows how to adapt the strategies to suit the stages each child has reached. By creating spirals for each child, teachers can then group according to similarities. Children with SEND are not automatically in the lowest group for every activity, although looking at some classrooms this would appear to be the case: with flexibility of grouping they can contribute to a range of activities dependent upon the learning objectives of the session. What teachers may have to adopt is a sensitivity to the impact they are having on all the children with the approaches they have chosen and the flexibility to adapt these to suit the range of children in the class.

Strategies that work well for all children

Social constructivist pedagogy

Social constructivist pedagogy involves using effective scaffolding and social interaction to reinforce learning. This is facilitated by effective partner and group working. Often teachers feel they are doing group work, but in fact they have children sat in a group doing their individual tasks. For group work to be most effective, the children need roles and the opportunity to work with other children who have different skills from them. Then all children in the group can enjoy success. With younger children, role-play areas encourage interaction – with effective adult intervention, these can be challenged to ensure learning as well as playing.

Play-based learning

Play is not exclusive to very young children. Providing a range of resources for older children to use to understand new mathematical concepts, or undertaking investigations in science will use the same characteristics of good play: open-endedness, opportunities for individual approaches, social interaction and communication.

Circle time

Circle time is an ideal opportunity to develop children's personal, social and emotional awareness and skills. Emotional literacy – the ability to express one's emotions and understand the impact those have on others – can be nurtured in circle time due to the confidential and supportive nature of the environment. The teacher can model the language of emotions, how one might manage emotions, and how to apply this knowledge to interaction with others.

Task 7.4   Including diverse learners

You have two children in your class who you are worried about including in group work in maths lessons. One of the children is working at a significantly later developmental stage than the others in the class so often works alone (some would refer to this child as mathematically 'gifted'), while the other has Asperger's Syndrome and is developmentally advanced in maths but struggles to work with the other children in the class. You want to help these children to work in groups, to develop their problem-solving skills with other children and to use the talents of other children to enhance their own capability.

Figures 7.3 and 7.4 show personal, social and emotional spiral diagrams for the two children:

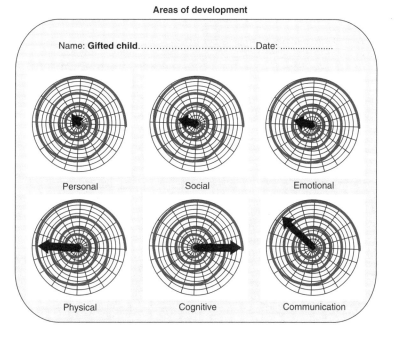

Figure 7.3   Gifted child's dashboard

(Continued)

(Continued)

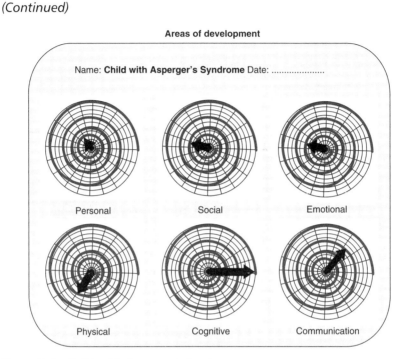

Areas of development

Name: **Child with Asperger's Syndrome** Date: ....

Personal   Social   Emotional

Physical   Cognitive   Communication

Figure 7.4   Child with Asperger's Syndrome

As you can see the spirals for both children are the same for PSED, although they could be very different on other areas of development. Also they could have different capacities to change the spiral spectrum diagrams for each area dependent upon their engagement with these activities and the nature of their special educational need.

Plan how you could work with these children to help them develop their group working skills in maths.

Table 7.4   Planning for maths

Action	How this would impact on pedagogy	How this would impact on children's development
Find the children partners for talking partners who are less well developed in maths, but sensitive.	Talking partners benefits all the children. These pairs would benefit the children who were less developed in their mathematical	Both children would have to be sensitive to the needs of the child less confident in maths – learning not just to give the answer, but also to have a

(Continued)

(Continued)

Action	How this would impact on pedagogy	How this would impact on children's development
	ability, as they would have a child/teacher and the focus children would be encouraged to talk.	discussion with the child about why an answer was correct – this is a non-threatening way to encourage them to talk.

Discuss your ideas with your peers – what have they observed in their placements that could be useful here?

Summary

In this chapter we have looked at how PSED emerge as separate areas and combine in children's ability to understand themselves and others. Through an understanding of theorists related to social development and how social interaction links to learning, we have examined the strategies that you can use in your teaching. We have applied the Spiral Spectrum Model to PSED and considered what the model can provide in terms of information related to identification of need and teaching.

Additional resources

Palaiologu, I. (2009) *Childhood Observation*. Exeter: Learning Matters.
Although this text includes material from previous political administrations, the ideas related to effective observation of 3 to 5 year-olds can be used when observing children across the primary age phase.

www.gov.uk/early-years-foundation-stage
This website outlines the Early Years Foundation Stage curriculum for children from birth to age 5. It includes developmental stages with ideas for how to support children at early stages of development. It can be helpful in finding strategies for children at early stages of development at ages before and beyond 5.

CHAPTER 8

COMMUNICATION, LANGUAGE AND LITERACY DEVELOPMENT

Learning Objectives

After engaging with this chapter you will be able to:

- Understand the complexity of communication, language and literacy development.
- Consider how to create a language-rich learning environment.
- Examine the needs of children across the learning spectrum in communication, language and literacy.

Introduction

In this part of the book we are considering the practicalities of being a teacher in an inclusive classroom through focusing on how to respond to diverse stages of development among individuals within a class group. By examining areas of child development, we are able to consider the needs of all children who fluctuate along the spectrum of development. A child does not have to have a disability or special educational need to have life experiences that cause differences in language processing and use. In this chapter we explore the various needs of children in terms of communication, language and literacy. These include children who cannot or do not speak; children for whom processing language is challenging; and children who come from families where there is not a language-rich environment, as well as those with a recognised need such as dyslexia and language learning delay.

Definitions

Language development has several strands:

- Hearing language and processing what is heard to create meaning.
- Speaking language that is at an appropriate level of complexity and meaning.
- Reading language and making meaning from what is read.

Processing language is a complex activity involving hearing or reading words and being able to make meaning from them and responding appropriately. In a classroom, this could be evident from exchanges such as teachers providing the instructions for the lessons and a child's ability to follow these instructions. Often a teacher will expect the children to follow a complex series of multiple instructions without additional scaffolding. There are several reasons why a child may not be able to do this, but language processing is one of them. For some children language processing difficulties may result in just 'hearing' the final instruction, or they may find that long instructions are heard as 'white noise' rather than separate words after a while which makes identifying the individual instructions too challenging. Imagine trying to put together flat pack furniture with all the instructions muddled up and written without pictures. Some people would still be able to make a good effort at making the item, others would need the pictures and the instructions in order to complete it accurately. For children with language processing difficulties, the pictures and instructions are required.

Spoken language involves structural processes, vocabulary and organisation of words. Structural processes involve the correct formation of letters and words using the tongue and mouth position. Some children have delay in structural formation of letters because they have a temporary hearing condition such as glue ear at a significant developmental stage so they cannot hear sounds correctly. This therefore means that they cannot discern the sounds they make and do not recognise when they are forming these incorrectly: as a result they do not learn to speak as clearly as they could. Immature formation of the muscles and placing of the tongue can also result in children substituting 'w' for 'r' and lisping on the 's' sound. Generally these improve as a child matures and gains control of the muscles and tongue.

Translating a grapheme into a phoneme and giving it meaning relies on several layers of knowledge before a child can finally be said to be reading for meaning. Decoding is the first stage and one which is relatively straightforward with a grounding in phonics, but decoding does not automatically lead to meaning. English is not a totally phonic language however, so there are soon exceptions to the rules a child learns and these can create complexity when moving beyond basic reading. A combination of phonics and picturing common irregular words therefore leads to a child being able to access literature. This is where language acquisition meets cognitive development. Children are ready at different ages to tackle the complexities of reading and where decoding may occur fairly early comprehending what is being read is an even more cognitive process.

Influences on communication, language and literacy development

It surprises many early years practitioners how many children arrive at school with poor communication skills and a lack of experience of books. In particular children from low socio-economic status families find communication with very young children a challenge. Exchanges between parents and children can focus on instructional language rather than developing rich vocabulary. Children are not introduced to books and learn language from television-style communication. The youngest child in a family can also continue with their childish speech patterns for an extended period as they rely on one or two word phrases to be understood by family members. They then expect when they reach school that this will be accommodated by teachers and other children.

Due to families not interacting as effectively as they could, children who experience juvenile lisps and other physical difficulties with tongue location and mouth muscle use are not corrected, and this will lead to speech and language referrals once they reach school.

SEND and communication, language and literacy

Physical: lisp, stammer, muscle weakness: lisp, stammer and muscle weakness in very young children often improve with maturity. If these progress beyond the early years (age 5) the child will need speech and language therapy in order to have modelled the correct physical mouth and tongue location and breathing to overcome stammering.

Cleft lip or palate: operations to rectify a cleft lip or palate are generally completed early after birth. There can be residuary effects with early speech, but these can be supported via speech therapy.

Emotional: selective mutism is a conscious or emotional decision not to speak and can occur in children for a variety of reasons. It can be a response to abuse, but also a fear of new circumstances including starting school. In some children mutism affects all areas of sound making, including laughing and crying.

Receptive or expressive language difficulties: hearing impairment can be temporary (e.g. glue ear), or permanent (e.g. deafness) and language development relies on hearing speech correctly. If a child is partially deaf, for whatever reason, they will not hear words as they are supposed to be pronounced and so will not be able to repeat them. As well as hearing the sounds incorrectly, the child may also not hear their own voice accurately so will be unable to correct their speech.

The Spiral Spectrum Model and communication, language and literacy development

 ## Task 8.1   Using the Spiral Spectrum Model and dashboard

Look at the spiral spectrum dashboard for Emily below.

The Year 1 teacher has created this spiral dashboard for Emily aged 5. Emily is a bubbly character who is well liked by her peers. She is a compliant pupil and always appears to be listening well when sitting on the carpet for the introduction to lessons. Emily does not offer answers to questions asked during whole class sessions. When she is asked directly she can sometimes answer as if she has not been following. When Emily goes back to her table she does not do any work and appears to have forgotten what was said on the carpet. Her teacher assumes that she does not understand and is having difficulty with the concepts covered in the lessons. Emily often works one to one with a TA, and when she does this she can complete the work. Her teacher would like her to start working independently because she thinks she is becoming too dependent on the one-to-one support. Could there be another explanation for Emily's lack of work? Could the teacher have got the dashboard wrong? What could be the reason for the position of the arrows on the dashboard?

(Continued)

(Continued)

Areas of development

Name: **Emily** ....Date: ....

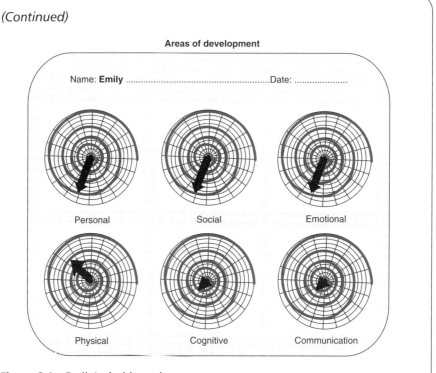

Personal	Social	Emotional
Physical	Cognitive	Communication

 Figure 8.1 Emily's dashboard

Reflection Point

Things to think about with regard to communication development:

1   Emily has been assessed as having low cognitive development and low communication development. These are not automatically linked. Emily could be having difficulties with receptive language. This means that when she is hearing the teacher's introduction, she is finding it challenging to process that information at the speed it is spoken. It does not mean that she could not understand the concepts, but that she will need additional scaffolding in order to be able to complete the tasks. So the teacher could provide her with a written version of what is being said in order that she can refer back to this at her own pace. Alternatively there could be a pictorial representation of the work expected if reading is still too challenging. Using either of these methods would help Emily to demonstrate her conceptual awareness and work more independently.

(Continued)

(Continued)

2 Emily may be having difficulty with expressive language. In other words, she understands what is going on, but finds it too challenging to locate and organise the words to respond. The teacher may not be providing enough time for Emily to find the words to answer. Next time you observe a teacher, count how many seconds children are given to answer questions – you will be shocked at how few it is. Then get the teacher to count how many seconds you give children to answer – this feels like a long time when you are teaching, but research suggests that teachers give children an average of three seconds to respond. Emily may need a lot longer than this. Thinking time and/or partner talk can be valuable strategies to help support Emily with formulating her thoughts.

3 If material is presented in a written format, it could be that Emily has difficulty forming meaning from the written word. This could be related to dyslexia. Children with dyslexia can be initially thought to be experiencing earlier cognitive development because they are not making the same progress as their peers with decoding written language. Emily would work better with pictures or with the spoken word as a demonstration of her understanding rather than words. Dyslexia is not linked to cognitive ability, so it is for the teacher to find alternative ways of supporting Emily expressing her knowledge.

These three alternative explanations for Emily's pattern of learning behaviour provide reasons why the teacher might have got the spiral dashboard incorrect, which leads to inappropriate learning strategies for her. However, it is easy for teachers to misinterpret the evidence before them because learning is complex and children are not always able to tell you how they are learning. If Emily is experiencing one of the language difficulties above, her dashboard may look more like the one below (Figure 8.2) – which provides the teacher with a useful picture of how to proceed with her learning.

Looking at the new dashboard in Figure 8.2, we can see a different picture of Emily in relation to her peers. The spiral dashboard now shows that her 'bubbly character' may be to overcome some insecurities about not being able to express her understanding. Emily would benefit from understanding that her communication difficulties do not define her as a learner, they can be overcome through additional scaffolding and strategies that could benefit other children in the class. Now the spiral represents Emily's cognitive development as average but her communication as low.

Table 8.1 Emily: links to pedagogy

	Personal	Social	Emotional	Physical	Cognitive	Communication
What evidence is there for the arrow being where it is?		Emily is a bubbly character who is well liked by her peers.				
Do you have any questions about why the arrow is where it is?			If Emily is a bubbly character why wouldn't she want to answer questions on the carpet?			
What could be wrong about the arrows?	Perhaps Emily wants to work with the TA because she lacks self-esteem in which case her personal development would be low.					

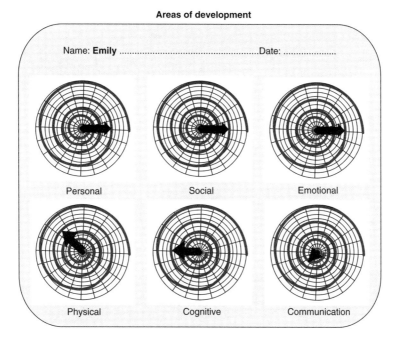

Figure 8.2   Emily and communication

The value of a spiral dashboard is that teachers can group children together who provide mutual benefit to each others' learning. In addition, teachers can create learning strategies that will benefit children across the class. It helps the perception of children with different development profiles as on a spectrum of learning, not children who are typical and children who have special needs. Emily's learning, for example, can be supported in ways that are beneficial to all children, so why consider her as having 'special' needs? By perceiving Emily's communication challenges as a special need, the teacher originally assumed she was also earlier in her cognitive development – whereas, in fact, she was just struggling to communicate her knowledge.

Looking at the three dashboards below, which child would you sit next to Emily and why?

Shi Lin may seem like an obvious choice – she is at the high end of the cognitive development for her peers and the same for communication. This means that she would be able to complete the tasks set by the teacher, so Emily could be modelled the right answer. However, Shi Lin has immature social and emotional development compared to her peers – this might result in her not being able to work well with Emily who would need more patience during group work and time to formulate her

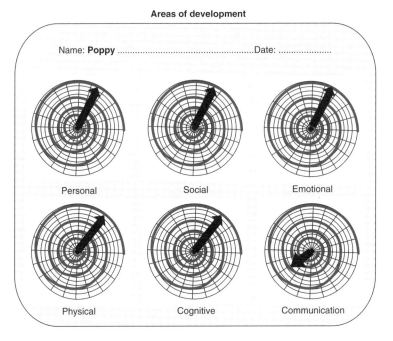

Figure 8.3 Partners for Emily: Poppy

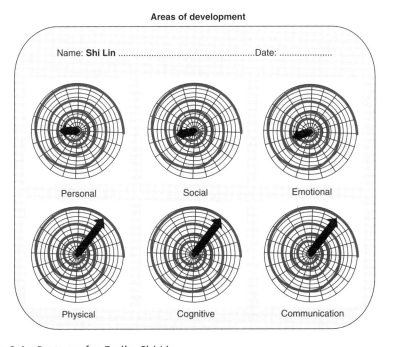

Figure 8.4 Partners for Emily: Shi Lin

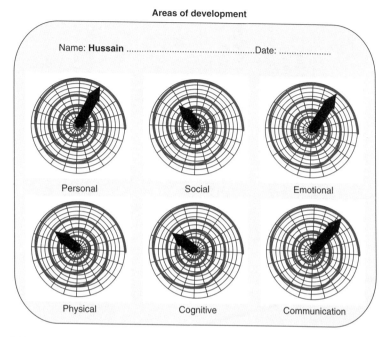

Figure 8.5   Partners for Emily: Hussain

contribution. So what about Poppy, who shares Emily's profile for communication development? She is also mature in cognitive development and social development – wouldn't that be ideal for empathising with Emily? Perhaps not, as Poppy and Emily would both find it challenging to communicate their understanding. However, this may be for different reasons and they may not be able to support each other's communication challenges. So I would choose Hussain. He has average to above average social and emotional development compared to his peers, and the same level of cognitive development as Emily, but a mature level of communication development for the class. With this balance Hussain should be able to support Emily with her communication difficulties, but she would have something to offer with knowledge and understanding of the task.

A well-considered set of spiral dashboards, together with an understanding of the children involved, can help teachers plan their classroom organisation for the whole class as well as planning interventions and learning strategies for individual children. Supporting this process is an awareness of why a child may have lower development than their peers in particular areas. Below are some of the theories presented as to how communication, language and literacy develop. Theories provide an added ingredient for teachers for their consideration of how to meet all children's needs.

Table 8.2 Communication theorists

Theorist	Theory related to communication, language and literacy development	Relationship to pedagogy
Noam Chomsky (1928–)	Put forward the notion that there is a language acquisition device whereby humans are programmed to acquire spoken language. They pick up general grammatical rules for speech and although in English they make errors these are due to the exceptions and over application of given rules.	Children may not recognise language errors just through hearing correct speech and they cannot automatically apply spoken language to writing and reading. Modelling good speech is essential, but so is applying this to writing so that children can recognise the relationship between speaking and writing.
David Crystal (1941–)	At around eight months old children sound the same across different nationalities and it is after this that children learn intonation from their language specifically. From there come words which hold meaning. There is a structured way in which language is acquired which is common across children even though it is acquired at different rates with different children.	
Jerome Bruner (1915–)	At the Iconic stage (age 1 to 7 years) children create images of what they are learning. At the Symbolic stage (age 7 years plus), children represent learning through symbols and codes which include language.	If you have children within the Iconic stage, supporting their learning with pictures, video etc. could provide additional reinforcement. This provides a foundation for when language begins to become more symbolic.

So what is effective pedagogy for communication, language and literacy development? What is a language-rich learning environment?

'Language-rich' relates to the modelling of spoken and written language, opportunities to practise language, the celebration of home languages, recording voices and opportunities to perform. In a language-rich learning environment you would see words for labelling, supporting writing, topic-related vocabulary, multi-lingual labels and instructions, language challenges etc.

Communication pedagogy comprises constant modelling through books, conversation, interaction and performance. Communication has to be an active process, where children are participants in their own learning. Social constructivist learning where children learn from each other in role play, group work, problem solving and the like, will provide the foundations for language which goes on to develop into abstract thought and communication.

 ## Task 8.2   Creating a communication web

When you are next in school, observe a group of children completing a group activity. Create a communications web like the one in Figure 8.6:

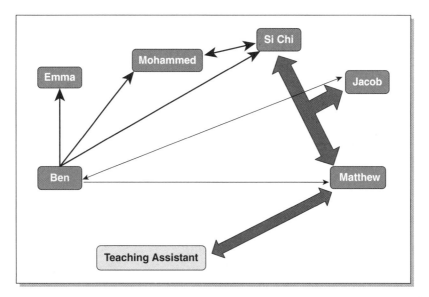

Figure 8.6   Communication web (basic)

What is this communication web telling you?

Look at the direction of the arrows and how thick they are. Bearing in mind this is supposed to be a group activity, how successful do you think this would be with the children communicating in this way? What does the web potentially tell you about the children's abilities in communicating?

Ben looks to be the leader of the group. He talks to each of the other children. But only one child communicates back – why might this be? It could be that he is not respected as a leader. Or it could be that he is so well considered by the children that they do as he says without the need for further explanation or question.

Emma has not said anything. Is this because she is distracted, has nothing to contribute, or is working on her own? Again, this is not the best model of group working, but we don't see from the communication web why this is the case.

Si Chi, Jacob and Matthew share a lot of talk. It would seem at first glance that they are collaborating well. But Matthew has also interacted a lot with the TA. Is this because he is reliant on a lot of support before he can participate?

Now add to the initial communication web to indicate how successful the activity was:

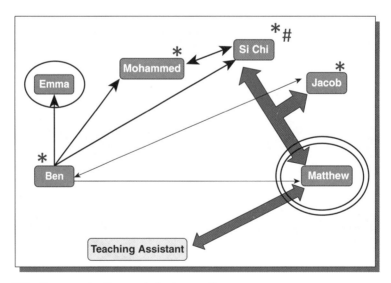

Figure 8.7   Communication web (enhanced)

Key:
Working well towards the identified task *
Working well within own ability *#
Working on own towards the identified task ◯
Needing a lot of one-to-one support to complete the task ◯

Now what is this communication web telling you?

Ben, Jacob and Mohammed are communicating well and working towards the task. Jacob is trying to get Si Chi and Matthew involved even though they are not as able to complete the task as he is. Jacob is, therefore, showing high levels of communication development as well as high personal and social development.

Now see if you can complete their spirals for communication based on the communication web.

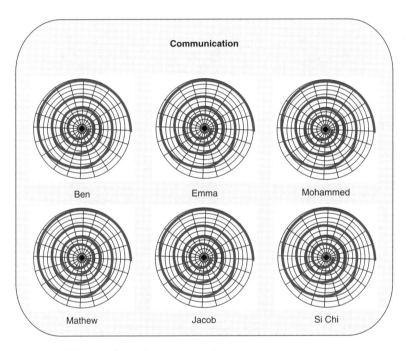

Figure 8.8 Dashboards linked to communication web

Remember that as you complete the spirals you are thinking about the range of skills in communication, i.e. processing language – understanding what you have heard and being able to understand what it means. This would be evident in those children who were able to understand the teacher's instructions and complete them, i.e. spoken language – being able to express your ideas to others so they can understand what you are saying.

In order for communication to be effective, it also needs to blend with social development. In this group work activity Emma may have good communication skills, but she is not using them as she is focused on her own work. She shows cognitive ability by completing the task, but there is not the evidence to demonstrate her communication development.

You would need further evidence to complete the spiral accurately. So, do your spirals look like mine below?

Using the evidence above this is what I would do to create a comparison between the children in the activity:

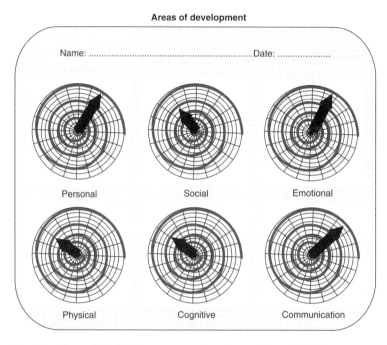

Figure 8.9 Dashboards linked to communication web modelled

Communication, language and literacy development and special educational needs

How to work effectively with a child who is mute

Children who are mute do not flourish in an environment where they are humiliated or their difficulty is highlighted in front of their peers. Other ways of communicating need to be found so that the child can join in the learning. The best way to include children who are mute is to include all children in the same activity. For example, using whiteboards to present answers altogether can enable children who do not like or are unable to speak to answer. This also supports effective formative assessment. Finding a buddy for a mute child can support any willingness they have to whisper or communicate non-verbally. Partner work in this way provides an opportunity for the mute child to contribute without the pressure to perform.

How to support a child with a lisp or a stammer

The ideas above can be useful for children with a lisp or stammer as well as those who are mute. Performance, reading aloud and answering in whole class sessions are all highly challenging circumstances for these children. If children are required to answer, they also require time and patience. Children in the class need to learn to respect the time that a child needs to answer. Neither you as the teacher, nor the children, should finish a child's sentence or words as this draws more attention to the child's difficulties. Speech and language therapists will provide exercises and ideas for supporting the child which will need to be carried out regularly as directed.

Summary

Communication is a complex area of development as it incorporates various elements of operational and conceptual skills and abilities. The Spiral Spectrum Model supports this complexity by identifying strengths in other areas such as personal, social and emotional development that create a more rounded picture of a child's profile that would impact on communication. We have also explored how it is easy to be misled by evidence in a classroom when the focus is on measurable outcomes (i.e. written work). It is easy as a teacher to become focused on the finished article of a lesson, rather than how children are trying to get there. Use of the communication web and the spiral spectrum dashboard helps us discover the children's journey through learning.

Additional resources

www.bdadyslexia.org.uk/
The British Dyslexia Organisation provides information and activities for children with dyslexic tendencies and can also supply valuable information for similar areas of communication.

www.communication4all.co.uk/HomePage.htm
These are educational resources for communication development.

www.ican.org.uk
A charity website for children with communication disorders.

CHAPTER 9

PHYSICAL DEVELOPMENT

Learning Objectives

After engaging with this chapter you will be able to:

- Gain an understanding of gross and fine motor skills development.
- Consider the links between physical development and other areas of development.
- Meet children's individual physical needs in the classroom.
- Apply the Spiral Spectrum Model in ways that enable effective personalised responses to diversity in physical development.

Introduction

A child cannot ride a bike.

A child cannot do up their shoelaces.

A child's handwriting is illegible.

Do all of these things automatically indicate special educational needs or disabilities in terms of physical development? In this chapter we will be examining the range of reasons for diversity in physical development. As a practitioner, it is your responsibility to create a learning environment where all the physical needs of children are supported in order for them to access the broad curriculum. Have a think about the examples above and all the potential reasons why these may be the case. We will be revisiting them later in the chapter. Most importantly, how would you work with children in these circumstances? The purpose of this chapter is to help you answer this question.

Defining physical development

Physical development falls into two categories – *gross motor* and *fine motor* development. Gross motor development is, literally, large motion. Developmentally, the first area of concern is gross motor. Parents are presented with charts that indicate 'typical' development so will monitor the first time a baby can hold their head up, sit unaided, crawl etc. Although children may develop these skills at different times, the general milestones are monitored by health visitors and doctors as there are key skills a child should be able to show within a timescale to ensure their ongoing successful fine motor and cognitive development. Fine motor development relates to smaller motions that require more control. For example, pincer movements with the fingers (which initially relate to children being able to do things such as stack blocks) develop later into holding a pencil.

Influences on physical development

It may seem that nothing would have an impact on physical development – children just grow and learn to control their gross and fine motor skills. However, from before birth there are impacts on growth and control. Before birth a mother's diet, whether she smokes or drinks, and whether she takes drugs or not, will influence a child's development after they are born. Babies can be born early or at a very low birth weight and this can influence development for years. A low birth weight can affect cognitive as well as physical development, which then impacts on learning. There is also research to suggest that a very low birth weight is related to the development of ADHD, anxiety and mood disorders.

SEND: physical development

Dyspraxia

Dyspraxia is a developmental coordination disorder. It is characterised by a lack of coordination, challenges with organisation and planning, and carrying out movements. Previously known as clumsy child disorder, dyspraxia affects gross and fine motor skills. However, it can also impact on other areas of organisation and planning such as remembering to bring resources to school and losing things. Dyspraxia is not linked to cognitive ability.

Cerebral palsy

Cerebral palsy is generally identified within the first three years of life and is characterised by muscle weakness, weak tone, loose limbs or stiffness, and occasional uncontrolled movements. The condition varies in severity but does not affect cognitive ability. As with dyspraxia, the impact of cerebral palsy on a child's coordination and physical aptitude can affect their self-esteem and confidence.

Cystic fibrosis

With cystic fibrosis a child's lungs fill with mucus and can result in a persistent cough and poor physical development. The condition can be managed but is incurable. Repeated lung infections cause further physical difficulties throughout childhood. Teachers need to understand how cystic fibrosis affects the individual child so that they can plan for their inclusion in physically demanding lessons.

Physical disability

Physical disabilities include sensory disabilities – hearing impairment, visual impairment – and any physical impairment as a result of an accident or impairment at birth. Sensory impairments will require some specialist input, but there is no reason why physical impairments would impact on cognitive development. However, there is a requirement for teachers to have a good understanding of the child's abilities so that these can be included in the broad curriculum. Physical disability accounts for less than 5% of the population of children with special educational needs, but can vary in intensity across the whole spectrum of abilities and impairments.

Muscular dystrophy

Muscular dystrophy is a progressive condition and can be life limiting. It results in a gradual weakening of the muscles. There are various types of muscular dystrophy that can affect different groups of people and at different levels of severity. Physiotherapy can be part of the management process of the condition, but so can medication such as steroids that have significant side effects including weight gain, muscle weakness and easy bruising. These will also have an impact on how a child with muscular dystrophy will be able to access a physical curriculum.

Spina bifida

In spina bifida the child is born without the spinal column having fully closed, exposing nerves. This results in the necessity for an operation to close the column. The resulting nerve damage can cause paralysis in the lower limbs, incontinence and a loss of sensation. Before including a child with spina bifida in physical curricular activities, a teacher would need to understand the impact of spina bifida on the child (see www. nhs.uk/conditions).

The Spiral Spectrum Model and physical development

The dashboard in Figure 9.1 and Table 9.1 relate to a child called Sam.

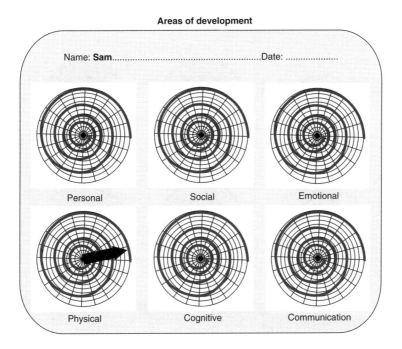

Figure 9.1   Sam's dashboard

Table 9.1 Implications of Sam's dashboard

	Gross motor skills	Fine motor skills
What does the arrow on Sam's dashboard mean?		
If Sam was in Year 2 what would you expect him to be able to do?		
What would be your expectations in Year 6?		

What difference does this mean to learning for Sam?

Perhaps he will be good at PE, have neat handwriting, but what about learning? For this you need to examine the whole of Sam's dashboard.

Have a look at the two dashboards in Figures 9.2 and 9.3 that differ only in physical development – what different strategies would you use for the two children when it comes to learning to tell the time in Year 2?

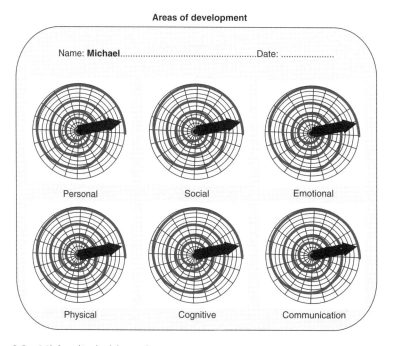

Figure 9.2 Michael's dashboard

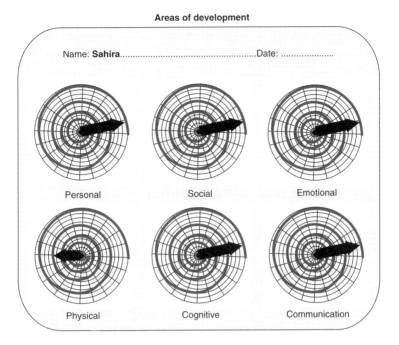

Figure 9.3 Sahira's dashboard

Out of the following strategies, which ones would suit Michael and which Sahira?

1. Using small clocks and manipulating the hands to show the time.
2. Drawing hands on pictures of clocks.
3. Working in a group to order clocks with different times.
4. Writing the time underneath pictures of clocks.
5. Using a large hoop and numbers to create a clock on the floor.
6. Cutting and pasting pictures of clocks.

Michael may learn via 1, 2 and 6, and Sahira with 3, 4, 5 – why might this be so? Michael has fine motor control so he can manipulate the hands on small clocks easily and for the same reason would find drawing the hands on pictures of clocks manageable. Drawing the hands on the clocks requires an ability to draw one hand longer than the other and for the hands to be positioned correctly (i.e. the difference in the long hand position between o'clock and half past). This fine motor control may be too challenging for Sahira. Her lack of fine motor control may lead to her having her work marked incorrect when she can visualise the correct alignment but is unable to control her pencil well enough to draw it. She would be better with writing, working in a group, and a good whole class activity like making a clock out of a hoop and large hands and numbers. This way she can demonstrate her understanding of time without her physical development challenges getting in the way.

 Task 9.1   Try it for yourself – responding to diversity in physical development

Let's go back to the introduction and the children we met:

- A child cannot ride a bike.
- A child cannot do up their shoelaces.
- A child's handwriting is illegible.

What could the reasons be for this and what impact would it have on learning?

So how do teachers support the physical development of children, as surely it is more important to focus on cognitive or communication development? Kinaesthetic approaches to learning, however, have been seen to have more impact on memory and the ability to apply learning to problem solving or practical applications. Children start their learning kinaesthetically – as babies they learn about objects by putting them in their mouths, they manipulate objects in play that help them develop spatial awareness. Play is the key to developing this area of development. Children of all ages need to play to explore new learning. Whether that play is in a nursery setting or doing a science experiment in Year 6, the physical manipulation of materials, the freedom to try different methods of approach, the opportunity to make mistakes in a supportive environment will help children to learn and for that learning to become concrete.

The theories related to play and its impact on learning can help teachers provide the experiences and alternative learning strategies a child needs to reinforce knowledge and understanding that pure 'book learning' would fail to do (see Table 9.2: also www.montessori.org.uk and www.steinerwaldorf.org/steiner-education).

Table 9.2 Physical development implications

	Reason 1		Reason 2		Reason 3	
	SEND	Impact on learning	Life experiences	Impact on learning	Global learning delay	Impact on learning
Cannot ride a bike			Child has never ridden a bike. Family cannot afford one			
Cannot do up their shoelaces						Poor hand/eye coordination may have an impact on other areas of fine motor control, spatial awareness, perspective
Child's handwriting is illegible	Dyspraxia					

Table 9.3 Play theorists

Theorist	Theory related to play and physical development	Relationship to pedagogy
Maria Montessori (1870–1952)	Montessori approached the education of young children through scientific investigation in her role as a doctor. She supported the idea that children learned through the manipulation of objects in an organised and deliberate way. She believed in the creativity of children and their ability to develop understanding without the constant instruction of teachers.	Whilst mainstream primary schools would not have Montessori provision resources, it is possible to be informed by the theory that children have an innate creativity that can be exploited in their active discovery of new knowledge. This links physical activity with cognitive activity – kinaesthetic learning.
Friedrich Froebel (1782–1852)	• Recognition of the uniqueness of each child's capacity and potential. • An holistic view of each child's development. • Recognition of the importance of play as a central integrating element in a child's development and learning. • An ecological view of humankind in the natural world. • Recognition of the integrity of childhood in its own right. • Recognition of the child as part of a family and a community. (See www.froebeltrust.org.uk/history.html)	Again play is a significant feature of learning. Learning from the Froebel approach, you can appreciate the involvement of the environment in learning, particularly the physical world. Physical interaction with the natural world has the potential to enhance learning, particularly for children who find formal classroom learning a challenge.
Rudolf Steiner (1861–1925)	Steiner education balances creativity with physical and intellectual development. In Steiner education the focus is on integrating all areas of development at an age-appropriate level. Movement, drama, outdoor learning are all integral parts of the learning process, ensuring a kinaesthetic engagement with the curriculum.	How will an awareness of Steiner education enable you to provide a more holistic way of learning for children in your class? Outdoor learning does not feature highly in upper primary teaching – how could it help develop a better understanding of the curriculum?

So what is effective pedagogy for physical development?

Physical development is far more than PE lessons and outdoor play. Consider both elements – fine motor skills and gross motor skills, and the creativity of physical play.

Gross motor skills develop first and as a teacher you will need to be aware that some children will not have had the same opportunities to refine their gross motor skills. In early years settings there need to be opportunities for crawling, climbing and cycling as these lead to more refined skills later on. Crawling utilises both sides of the brain and improves coordination. Peddling again requires children to apply opposite pressures at the same time. These skills become useful when a child learns to do such things as typing, where the hands need to operate simultaneously but in different ways. Ultimately, driving will draw on all of these skills.

How often do physical development aspects feature in success criteria for lessons other than PE for year groups after the early years?

In my experience, very rarely. In a maths lesson, you could include a success criterion that relates to the correct formation of numbers as well as subject-related criteria. During the lesson, one of the aspects of support input could be to check that children are seated correctly and holding their pencils correctly to achieve this criterion. There is an immense amount to remember as you teach maths, but if you also remember to guide children frequently with such things as posture and pencil grip it will become an automatic muscle memory.

Kinaesthetic learning suits children who need to manipulate materials in order to problem solve learning. Children are capable of selecting the resources they require for a given task if they are given the opportunity. So, on occasion, you should provide a range of resources on the children's tables or within reach so they can choose the method they will use for the task. We make assumptions about what makes a task easier but children do not necessarily develop sequentially, so providing them with opportunities to select enables them to engage metacognitively – namely to identify why they have worked out the problem the way that they have.

Theorists talk of visual, auditory and kinaesthetic learners. I do not hold that children only utilise one of these to learn effectively. As we have seen, play is effective for learning at all ages. It is not exclusive to so-called kinaesthetic learners. Children learn through multiple stimuli – visual, aural and physical: they may make preferences for the materials and methods they use, but generally a multi-sensory approach provides the best approach for effective learning.

Physical development and special educational needs

How can a child in a wheelchair join in with PE?

In 2012 the London Paralympics made large inroads in public opinion about disabled athletes. What had often been presented as a charity model of SEND – those poor people who are so brave – became a respect for athletes at their physical peak. Some of the sports, such as wheelchair rugby, also became very popular due to their intensity and physical challenge. Wheelchair users were not viewed as weak and impaired, but strong and fierce competitors. Coverage of the games also challenged perceptions and the public were encouraged to raise questions about how to correctly describe disability. Similar to public perception about adult wheelchair users, child wheelchair users are much overlooked as individuals in the mainstream classroom. Schools were supported in adapting the physical environment to accommodate wheelchairs and children had funding where additional support workers were required. However, including children in the broad curriculum has not been so successful. Teachers want to include children, but are afraid that they will get things wrong.

Task 9.2   Let us consider a PE lesson

You are planning to do 'over and under' using gymnastic apparatus.
    You have a child in your class who is paralysed from the waist down. How can you include him? Firstly, you need to know the child – what physical movement is possible? How easily do they get tired? Then if they have a support worker, you must give them a chance to practise

(Continued)

(Continued)

some of the skills before they would have to repeat them in a whole class session. Once you have a good understanding of the child's limits and abilities, you can include them in planning.

You could have all children moving snake-like to start with, which is an inclusive activity. You could provide soft obstacles that the children could drag themselves over as well as more challenging apparatus that might exclude the child. The idea is not to reduce the challenge for all children, but to offer a graduated challenge that includes everyone.

How does dyspraxia affect learning and what can teachers do to help?

Adam arrives at school without his PE bag – he is sure he had it when he left home, but in fact he left it in the hall as he was going through the front door. He is tired because he had nightmares last night that woke him. He feels disheartened as he enters the classroom as he has already failed to bring his PE kit and now he is told that the first activity is writing. He has great ideas, but his handwriting is illegible even when he tries very hard. After writing he has to sit on the carpet with the rest of the class for an introduction to maths. He is concentrating so hard on keeping his back straight and his legs crossed that he misses most of what the teacher says. Every time he concentrates on her, he slumps in his place and gets told off for not sitting up. He is very good at maths and manages to work out what to do when he gets to his place, but instead of praise for the work he gets more criticism for his writing and the fact that his work seems to smudge easily as his non-writing hand moves across the page. After lunch – which he doesn't really eat much of, not really enjoying the sensation of eating and finding a knife and fork challenging – he has to borrow PE kit again. Oh no – laces! He cannot tie laces and several friends laugh at him for being so clumsy. A good friend helps out to stop the laughing. PE is torture – somehow when he concentrates on what his legs are doing, his arms go out of control; balance is difficult and catching requires too challenging hand/eye coordination. During the last session of the day the fire alarm goes off for a drill and Adam starts to cry. The overwhelming sound is just too much after all the other challenges of the day and he sadly follows his peers out of the classroom.

Dyspraxia has been called the invisible disability because it is complex, but has symptoms that are often mistakenly considered the child's fault, like the handwriting and the slumping, the forgetfulness and the lack of being able to tie laces. The condition is not related to intelligence, but many children are put in groups of children with special educational needs because their work is not neat, or they have struggled with concentration.

 Reflection Point

Let's go through Adam's day and see what could have been different:

1 *PE bag* – what about asking if he could have a spare kit in school? That way he gets a lot of praise if he does remember to bring the kit himself, but there is a back-up plan as well.
2 *Tired* – children with dyspraxia can have a tendency for nightmares. In the morning the teacher could just check in with Adam and do a quick thumbs up/down and if he is tired: bear this in mind for concentration in class.
3 *Writing* – children with dyspraxia can share dyslexic children's struggles to organise their thoughts before committing them to paper. Perhaps Adam could record his ideas in a brainstorm and then sequence them before starting to write.
4 *Handwriting* – laptops can help here as, and although writing may be slower, it is at least legible.
5 *Sitting on the carpet* – children with dyspraxia need support. This could be provided by leaning against a wall or a bean bag. This then allows them the opportunity to focus all their concentration on listening.
6 *Eating* – children with dyspraxia can get bored of the process of eating and give up. They may lack enjoyment in food and need encouragement to complete a meal. Packed lunches can help here as these could include different textures of food and different tastes.
7 *Laces* – shoes with Velcro fastening are less challenging.
8 *Gross motor skills* – because a child with dyspraxia can often only concentrate on one gross motor skill at a time, PE needs to be planned so that they can enjoy success in one skill at a time.
9 *Loud noises* – the teacher needs to be aware of a child's overreaction to loud noises so that there could be ear protectors in class for circumstances such as fire drills.

Strategies that work well for all children

Task 9.3   Developing Physical Skills Through Play

Child A

Child B   **Child C**

Look at the three pictures above. What skills are the children developing? Why is play an effective means for children to develop these skills?

(Continued)

(Continued)

- Child A is demonstrating ...
- Child B is demonstrating ...
- Child C is demonstrating ...

Consider gross motor skills and fine motor skills. Why is hand/eye coordination of importance? How does play relate to learning? What would be the next step for each child?

Child A: is working on her fine motor skills through painting carefully within the outline she has created. She has freedom to create.

In the future this will develop into more skilled manipulation of tools including pens and pencils, scissors etc. Creativity could develop into imaginative use of words and drama, and not just drawings. Freedom of expression can lead to an ability to 'think outside the box' and find alternative solutions to problems.

Child B: is demonstrating hand/eye coordination. Catching a ball is a challenging skill for young children that relies on their being able to watch the object coming towards them and move their hands into the right position for catching without watching them. Children are initially used to watching their hands and not the object, so this is a development of an early skill. In the future this will develop into tying laces, typing on a computer, driving, sport. This sort of play utilises both sides of the brain, which is valuable in problem solving and creative thinking.

Child C: is manipulating objects and engaging in imaginative play.

So is play just for young children? Does kinaesthetic learning end after the early years? Can the skills learned in early years play still contribute to learning as we get older? As the pictures demonstrate, elements of play, group activity and physical materials can support problem solving with older children.

Summary

Physical development can be one of the least well-understood areas of development because it is viewed as something that happens in PE. Teachers can fear doing the wrong thing for children with a physical disability, which results in their abilities being overlooked. We talked in

(Continued)

(Continued)

Part One of the book about focusing on the abilities of children with special educational needs rather than disabilities and this is a key element of meeting the needs of children with physical delays.

Play has been included in this chapter as a key way to address the kinaesthetic aspects of learning. It is also important in linking physical development with other development areas such as personal, social, emotional and communication. This combining of areas of development provides holistic learning opportunities in a less formal way. We have looked, briefly, at how these strategies do not need to apply solely to early years education (ages 3 to 5), but to life-long learning.

Additional resources

www.forestschools.com/
Forest school education supports physical development and learning through interaction with the practical outside world, and whilst not available to all schools, the principles of outdoor learning can be incorporated into mainstream primary education.

www.gov.uk/government/collections/improving-teachers-skills-in-sen-and-disabilities
This has DfE guidance on strategies for working with children with special educational needs.

CHAPTER 10

DRAWING IT ALL TOGETHER – HOW CHILDREN LEARN AND HOW WE TEACH INCLUSIVELY

Learning Objectives

After engaging with this chapter you will be able to:

- Draw together the theoretical and practical elements of the book in understanding children's learning.
- Understand the impact that an understanding of children's learning has on your teaching.
- Evaluate the value of implementing the Spiral Spectrum Model of difference in the classroom.

Introduction

In this book we have taken you on a journey from the development of special educational needs to its current position in primary education. This has been a political and social journey that has seen perceptions challenged by political necessities of funding and resourcing. Along the way we have asked you to reflect on your own perspective towards the education of those children who are identified as having special educational needs.

As we complete this part of the journey, we will draw the exploration of the different areas of development together in an overarching understanding of cognition and learning. We will also consider the value of using the Spiral Spectrum Model as a tool in the evaluation of children's individual development profiles and in adapting teaching to suit the holistic needs of the child.

An example from practice

In a school in Leeds, the spiral spectrum dashboard is used when referring a child for advice via the internal learning needs forum. The forum panel is the headteacher, deputy, targeted services officer and inclusion manager. Teachers may refer any child in their class who is of concern due to their learning progression, behaviour, change in circumstances or 'low' attainment. The dashboard is used to place the child across each of the areas of development comparative to their peers. This helps the teacher to analyse the children's needs and abilities beyond just the issue that caused them to make the referral. It also enables the panel to find helpful solutions. For example, if a child is at a very early stage of social development compared to their peers the panel may suggest a pairing as support rather than group work. If a child is at an earlier stage of communication compared to their peers the panel would suggest supportive activities that would work around the communication ability of the child whilst drawing on their relative developmental strengths. Teachers are finding the process of considering the range of development areas of the children valuable as previously they had just focused on what they considered was going wrong. Also the panel is recognising that it provides them with additional information prior to making suggestions about ways forward.

While the school will have the same pressures as any in the UK to meet official achievement targets, it recognises that achievement is not just a cognitive development issue but one that is also impacted upon by other areas of development. Therefore, teachers need help to utilise their awareness of these other areas to enable children to achieve to their full cognitive potential.

What do we know about cognitive development?

As inclusive teachers we have suggested that often you would not just consider a child's cognitive development, however it is a facet of development that does need to feature in a holistic review. We have left this until the final chapter in the book so that you would develop an awareness of how other features impact on achievement, but we do need to explore what cognitive development is and how it is measured.

Defining cognitive development

Cognitive development relates to how children learn. It is one of the most complex areas of development because the brain still has so many secrets. Cognitive development is not just about remembering facts, it is also about how a child can create connections between areas of learning, how they can apply learning to problem solving and how children can consider philosophical or intangible concepts. There has been much development in understanding the science of learning. In the image below we can see the dendrites that emerge as arms from the brain cell, firing electric impulses and joining other dendrites. We know now that the more connections are made the more secure the learning. As learning is reinforced these connections become stronger – the thicker dendrites are covered with a reinforcing 'coat' known as the myelin sheath, which prevents the connections from breaking. This chapter looks at the ways in which those connections can be reinforced and the different views on how learning is most successful.

It appears from this description that all children should learn in the same way. In terms of the brain cells, this is so. However, the strength of dendrite connection and the permanency of learning do

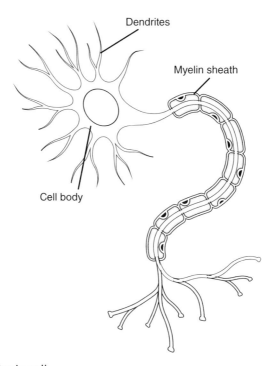

Figure 10.1 A brain cell

Source: Lyons et al. (2014), *Biological Psychology*, London: Sage.

differ. Understanding the science only takes us so far, and we need to understand the child to enable them to reach their potential.

Influences on cognitive development

Genetics

'Genes account for between approximately 50% and 70% of the variation in cognition' (Tucker-Drob et al., 2013). What this research is telling us is that while genetics can play a part in cognitive development, this does not give us the full story. A child's family circumstances can play an equal part in how that child's learning develops. This is important when teaching siblings. You may hear other teachers comment on whole families and make assumptions about a child based on how their older siblings have achieved. We learn here that, whilst it may be relevant, genetics cannot provide a simple answer to measuring a child's potential.

Family

Children who receive free school meals; who come from traveller, gypsy, Roma backgrounds; who are disadvantaged; who have special educational needs and who are white or black Caribbean perform less well than their peers. The 2012/13 initial statistics related to GCSE A*–C grades demonstrated that children on free school meals performed 20% less well than those not on free school meals; children from traveller, gypsy Roma backgrounds performed 50% less well; children with special educational needs 46% less than those without; and children from disadvantaged backgrounds 26% lower (DfE, 2014).

Working in early years settings in deprived areas, teachers can see the impact that socio-economic status can have on children's early development. Many children from these backgrounds enter school with little speech, regardless of whether English is their first language: children can also find interaction challenging and physically they can lack basic developmental skills. Lack of nutrition affects learning negatively and families without resources such as books and computers find that following up school learning at home can be difficult. These challenges can impact significantly on all other areas of development, so by creating a spiral spectrum dashboard you can identify individual needs and stages of development without devaluing these in relation to a 'norm' or placing limits on their capacity to progress.

SEND and cognitive development

Global learning delay

Children identified as having a global learning delay have a delay across several areas of development of generally at least 18 months. For young children this represents a significant proportion of their lives. Global delay means that children do not just have cognitive needs, but also communication, personal, social and emotional, and they can have physical development needs particularly in fine motor skills development. The pace of learning can also be slower than their peers, so what started as an 18-month delay can extend as they progress through school. Some schools will help to close this gap by having a child repeat Reception or Year 1 so that they have an opportunity to revisit the foundation curriculum. Generally with global delay this does not impact significantly on PSED in the same way it would with a child who just has cognitive delay.

The Spiral Spectrum Model and cognitive development

 ## Task 10.1　Evaluating the Spiral Dashboard for Cognitive Development

Look at the spiral below (Figure 10.2). Is this pattern of development possible? What does the dashboard tell you?

Literally the dashboard shows that this child is significantly less developed in personal, social, emotional, physical and communication development than their peers, but significantly more developed in cognitive development than their peers.

What do you know about the Spiral Spectrum Model and child development that will help you interpret what you can see?

Consider – how is the dashboard created? What are the inhibitors to development? If it is a comparative model what could be the issues that are causing this comparison?

Now decide – could this be an actual dashboard?

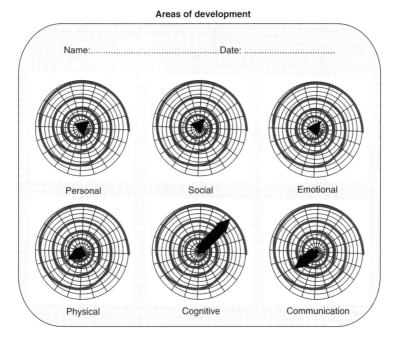

Areas of development

Name:..Date: ....

Personal   Social   Emotional

Physical   Cognitive   Communication

Figure 10.2   Cognitive development dashboard

The dashboard is possible. Let us think about why this is so and what you could do about it.

The main issue is evidence. To create the dashboard, teachers need evidence. Evidence can come from talking with family, schoolwork, talking with the child, interaction between the child and other children or adults, testing.

So how has this child produced the evidence for further cognitive development but not the others?

The confusing element is that communication development is at an earlier stage of development whereas cognitive development is at a significantly later stage.

Why might this be the case? Which of these could be the case?

1. English as an additional language.
2. Mutism.
3. Dyslexia.
4. Deafness.
5. Dyspraxia.

The answer? All of them or none of them. You would expect a child with an advanced level of cognitive develonment compared to their peers to also have high communication, ᵇ of our evidence as teachers is gathered through written or ᶜ communication. So let us consider how the above . result in this dashboard.

1. *English as an additional language:* the teacher could have presented the child with a test that did not rely on the English language (e.g. with pictures and numbers/symbols). So whilst in English they demonstrate poor communication, they were able to provide the evidence for conceptual understanding. It would have been better if the teacher had also been able to provide the child with an opportunity to demonstrate their understanding in their own language, to better measure their communication development. The dashboard, however, would change rapidly once the child starts to use the English language.

2. *Mutism:* this occurs for many reasons including emotional or other forms of abuse, fear of school, shyness or a severe lisp/stutter. Children with mutism may however be able to evidence abilities in written communication so will not need to be downgraded for this on the communication measure. This child could have demonstrated their cognitive understanding through schoolwork and tests that did not rely on the spoken word.

3. *Dyslexia:* this is a condition that is unrelated to intellectual capacity. It involves children having difficulty in decoding words and organising their own thoughts into the written word. There is usually a significant difference between a child's imagination and speech and what they can read or write (the debate related to dyslexia is presented in Chapter 5).

Key theorists for cognitive development

Understanding what theorists such as Vygotsky (Pass, 2004) say about how a child develops and learns can help teachers plan the next steps for children. In Part One you were encouraged to recognise that general learning theories and what is known about generally effective practice are more relevant for SEND than you might at first believe. Table 10.2 outlines some key theorists who have relevant theories for cognitive development.

Table 10.1   Cognitive development theorists

Theorist	Theory related to cognitive development	What else can you find out about this theory?	Relationship to pedagogy – over to you! Complete the table to decide how socially based learning theories impact on you as a teacher
Lev Vygotsky	Social Development Theory: Learning is based on interaction with others		
Jerome Bruner	Socio-Cultural Development: Learning takes place in a cultural context and is achieved through active interaction with others		
Albert Bandura	Social Learning Theory: Learning is achieved through observation of others and mimicking other behaviours		

So what is effective pedagogy for cognitive development?

Cognitive development is clearly most significant when it comes to the measures of achievement in our education system. Examinations at the end of Key Stages and the end of education are not measuring PSED, or in most cases physical development, so communication and cognitive evidence is needed to be able to express the child's potential. So, although we would advocate that teachers focus on all areas of development in the acquisition of knowledge, they also need to enable children to demonstrate that knowledge through a cognitive measure. To empower children in this way learning needs to relate to all areas of development so that whatever children learn is embedded. So how do you do this? You will need to plan lessons so that learning is addressed through physical engagement with materials; through opportunities for group interaction; and via opportunities to copy a model presented by the teacher and through a spiral approach, where children meet the same topics at a deeper level as they progress.

This involves understanding where the children are – through effective formative assessment. It also involves research into how a topic can utilise physical activities, the outdoors, group problem solving rather than always using a worksheet.

We have moved on from the need for a three-part lesson every time. You will need to consider the best organisation of time and resources to suit the material that you are delivering and the children's prior knowledge and experience. Not every lesson has to be 'fun', but all learning can be enjoyable and challenging. Children thrive on being able to learn and demonstrate their knowledge.

Task 10.2   Creating spiral spectrum dashboards for individual learners

Now that we have covered the six areas of development, see if you can create your own dashboard for the following children. Below is the sort of information you would be able to gather fairly simply from placement visits to school and conversations with teachers. The purpose of the task is to apply the skills you have been reading about in the previous four chapters and then consider the value of the graphic representation of comparison of development.

Mark and Adil are great friends, but very different. Adil is very shy and quiet, although he is happy to chat with Mark. Adil is the youngest of a large family; his brothers and sisters are quite a lot older than him and tend to treat him like a baby, even though he is now 6. Adil does not like working in a group, he prefers to quietly get on with his work and does not volunteer answers in whole class sessions, although he is very able. Mark is very confident and well liked by his peers. He can be described as naughty as he finds concentrating very difficult and is a wriggler on the carpet. Mark's communication skills are poor – he finds it difficult to organise his thoughts when he is speaking and when he does his written work.

Evie has a global learning delay of about two years compared to her peers. She is learning to speak, but not with new people. Evie generally repeats what she hears from others rather than formulate her own thoughts. She also tends to play on her own and does not show empathy for her peers when they get upset or hurt. She struggles to balance when using the play equipment and this also affects her fine motor control, not being able to confidently control a pencil. Mia is a caring child and she does a lot to help Evie in class, making sure she sits and listens in whole

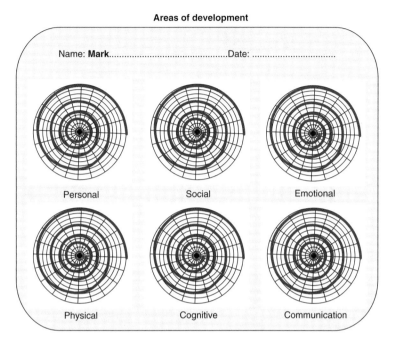

Figure 10.3 Assessing dashboards: Mark

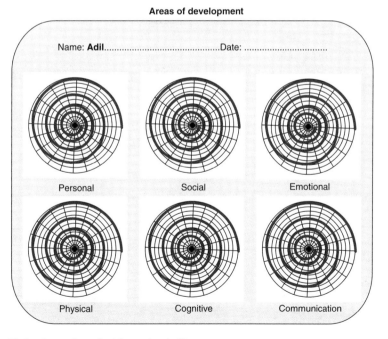

Figure 10.4 Assessing dashboards: Adil

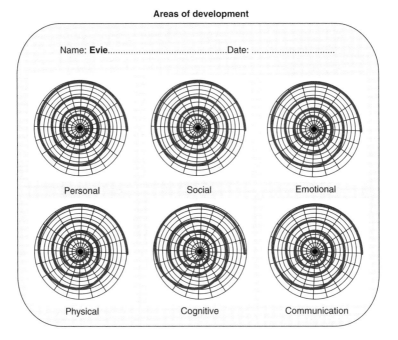

Figure 10.5 Assessing dashboards: Evie

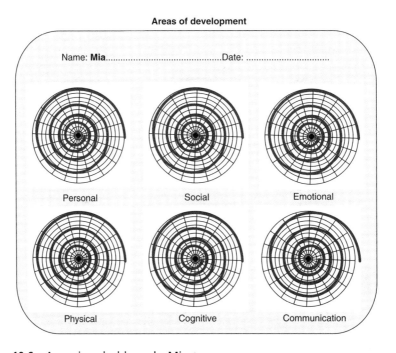

Figure 10.6 Assessing dashboards: Mia

class sessions. Mia is a mature child who is the oldest of three in her family and has a lot of caring duties at home. Mia is talented at maths, but finds literacy more difficult. She works hard to overcome any difficulties that she has had and is beginning to make good progress across the curriculum. It is suspected that she may have dyslexic tendencies. Mia's favourite activity is colouring and she is very careful with her pencil control.

Complete the spirals for each child using the information given above.

Task 10.3   Evie, Mia, Mark and Adil

In this description of a classroom activity you need to identify which of the four children (A, B, C and D) are Mark, Adil, Evie and Mia, and why you have decided on that particular order.

The children are engaged in a collaborative group activity, putting a story in order and then deciding on a new ending. Child A has a couple of the pictures in their hand and is looking at them. They say 'mine' and won't put them back on the table. Child B goes to Child A and encourages them to share the pictures between the two of them so the group can see what they are. Child C is moving the pictures around on the table in a random fashion, but helps Child D stick the pictures down when Child D and Child B decide on their order. A few minutes later the teacher reminds them that they have to also talk about a new ending to the story. Child A is playing with the scraps of paper that have been left after cutting the pictures out and is sticking them together. Child C is distracted, but gets involved in the conversation again when Child B starts talking about the task. Child B asks Child D to write down their ideas and reminds the group that they do not have much time. Child C offers ideas for what they should write, but these do not relate to a new ending but to the pictures they have already stuck down. Child A has now moved away from the group because Child B is concentrating on the task. By the time they have been told the lesson is over, the task has been completed by Child B and Child D, while the other two children are distracted and have lost track of the task.

Child A is …

Child B is …

Child C is …

Child D is …

Response: How did you create the spirals? Do they compare to the ones below?

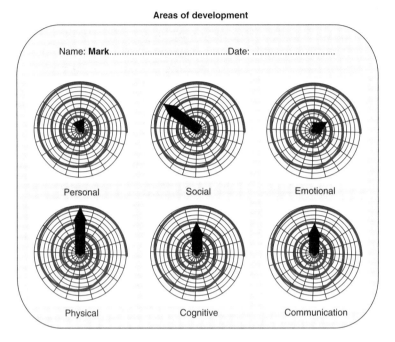

Figure 10.7   Assessing dashboards modelled: Mark

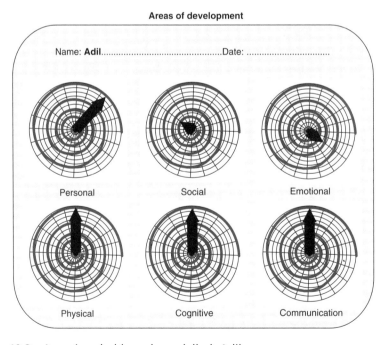

Figure 10.8   Assessing dashboards modelled: Adil

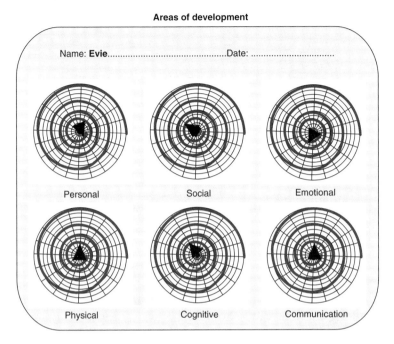

Figure 10.9   Assessing dashboards modelled: Evie

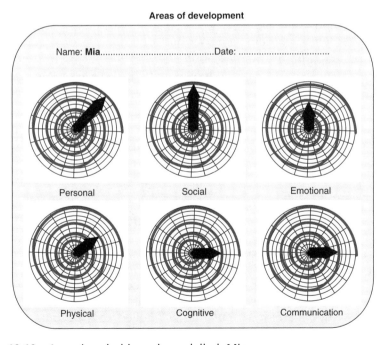

Figure 10.10   Assessing dashboards modelled: Mia

Read the lesson activity again. Do you still agree with your choices for which child is which?

Child A is Evie

Child B is Mia

Child C is Mark

Child D is Adil

Do you agree? What made you think that? How does knowing this help you with your teaching?

Knowing children's profiles helps you decide teaching strategies related to their cognitive stage of development. Mia, for example, demonstrates a more advanced stage of cognitive development but struggles to communicate her knowledge. Adil has cognitive development at a more advanced stage but would find group working a challenging way to demonstrate it. Evie is at an earlier stage of cognitive development and finds group working too challenging, so for her to demonstrate her awareness she would need one-to-one support and careful scaffolding of tasks. For Mia, this form of learning is probably a best fit. She is able socially, but finds writing her ideas difficult. For her, being able to use Adil's writing ability to represent her ideas was a best fit. Teaching is finding strategies that work for all children. So Evie could have worked in a group with a TA to enable her to participate to her best potential. Mark was doing well to keep participating in the task, but it was clear that he misunderstood the last element in it. He worked well with Adil and Mia, so was probably best placed in that group, and therefore differentiation could have been by outcome – in other words, expecting him to retell the story could have been enough for that day. He benefited from being with Adil and Mia who were able to complete the task, so perhaps next time he will be able to do a bit more.

 ## Task 10.3   Higher order questioning

At the beginning of the chapter we saw that the 'arms' coming from a brain cell need to join together with others for learning to take place. We also learned that for connections to become secure they need to develop a myelin sheath which acts like a coat. The myelin sheath only develops when learning is repeated or applied so it becomes deeper

(Continued)

(Continued)

and more likely to last. This is why we have a spiral curriculum in schools, repeating topics at a higher level each time we meet them, using the foundations embedded early in school to build on new understanding. But at the highest level of learning there is not just knowledge, but also the ability to apply that knowledge to challenging problems and analyses.

 Task 10.4   Developing understanding through effective questioning

When you are on a placement, observe a lesson and see how the teacher develops children's understanding through effective questioning.
    First complete the following tally chart:

Table 10.2   Tally chart 1

	0–5 minutes	6–10 minutes	11–15 minutes
Open questions: those that rely on a full answer			
Closed questions: those that can be answered with a simple yes or no			

Let us say it looks like the one below, so what would this tell you about the teaching?

Table 10.3   Tally chart 2

	0–5 minutes	6–10 minutes	11–15 minutes
Open questions: those that rely on a full answer		I	I
Closed questions: those that can be answered with a simple yes or no	ⅣↃ		II

(Continued)

(Continued)

How far can learning deepen with closed questions? These are useful for checking knowledge and recapping. But it is the open questions which challenge that knowledge and take a learner to a new level of understanding.

Look at the spirals below – both of these are for Sally. Two teachers created the spirals and then compared their outcomes. Why do you think they are so different?

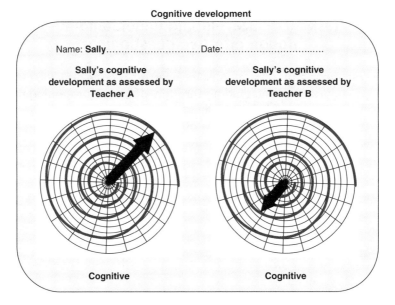

Figure 10.11 Sally's dashboard

Both the teachers are talking about the same class and the same child, so why are they so different?

You carried out an observation on the two teachers last week and this is the outcome of your observation:

Which teacher is which on your observation chart?

What is your reasoning?

You could argue for both teachers.

If Teacher A is the one who asked more open questions, she could have noticed that Sally was adept at applying her knowledge to problem-solving tasks and was becoming more analytical in her thinking, and therefore had developed further cognitively than her peers.

However, if Teacher A is the one who had asked more closed questions she might only be testing recall and Sally might be good at repeating facts but not at applying this knowledge. This would have presented Teacher A with a misunderstanding about Sally's cognitive development compared to her peers and Teacher B might have a more realistic view.

However, the point of the exercise is that the more information you have in making judgements about children's stages of development, including the sort of teacher you are, the more accurate those judgements will be.

Cognitive development summary

Our academic assessment system may rely on evidence of cognitive development, but as inclusive teachers we need to demonstrate our awareness that cognitive development does not occur in isolation and nor is it the be-all and end-all of what should be valued. It is by using an awareness of children's other areas of development that we will be able to ensure that all children reach their potential (incuding those with SENDs). We have seen throughout the previous chapters in Part Two of this book that there is a myriad of reasons why a child's development may not follow what many texts present as the typical or 'normal' route. These reasons are not all immediately apparent to a teacher as a child enters their class for the first time, but through careful examination of the evidence available through discussion with families, observation, classroom activities and previous education, it is possible to personalise learning without having children sit outside the general provision of the class in SEND groups.

We have endeavoured to show that teaching strategies linked to the holistic development needs of children do not have to be different for SEND, but a spectrum of strategies that will lead to inclusion for all. Inclusion is not just a term that relates to 20% of children identified with an SEND but to all children, who at one time or other throughout their education may feature in the earlier development areas of the spiral spectrum dashboard.

Journey's end?

Hopefully this text has supported you in your journey to becoming an inclusive teacher and challenged some previously held perceptions about ways to ensure inclusion for all in the primary classroom. We believe that the journey does not end here – the route map will continue throughout your career as new children enter your class and you learn new strategies for inclusion across the areas of development. For us, this has also been enriched by our experiences with our own children for whom the education system has sometimes presented more of a barrier than an enabler.

Sarah Trussler's son is registered blind. Her doctoral research was initiated by a primary teacher stating how worried they were about teaching him, even though this teacher was the Special Educational Needs Coordinator. To Sarah, her son was an ordinary boy, with a strong interest in football and above average academic ability. To the teacher he was a blind boy with special needs and requiring specialist teaching. She wanted to include him, but saw it as a hurdle. There is no denying that a child with a visual impairment needs some specialist input – learning Braille and typing for example – but his general education could happen in the same way as every other child's. As a parent Sarah had always told her son that his blindness was not an excuse. He still had to tidy his room, do his homework, help around the house and, as he got older, carry out volunteer work. Sarah recognised that in adult life her son would face barriers to work that other children would not, so she taught him resilience and he learned to find other ways to achieve the same things as his peers academically, in sport and in work. That teacher needed to find some alternatives for him by making his work bigger, but in all other ways he needed to be treated like other children. Otherwise he was getting the message that he was part of a special group that was not considered normal; other standards would apply to him, other staff would take him, he was not like his peers. By starting with the label 'blind', the teacher had adopted the view that this was a different child, a child who she may not be able to teach, a child who actually worried her; she was doubting her professional ability to meet his needs. If she had started from the perspective of 'boy', of above average ability, with the ability to communicate well verbally, who may need his work adapting, then that worry would not have existed.

Deborah Robinson's daughter has epilepsy, and its onset at age 14 challenged her teachers since she moved from being someone who found it easy to learn and remember to someone who found this incredibly difficult. Some of her teachers responded quickly to this and provided support (for example, extra processing time by building this into their usual teaching approach). Others stopped at the label 'epilepsy' and put all of her failures down to that whilst regarding its onset as a tragedy that they were unable to move past. In the end, she passed all of her GCSEs but in the subject areas where teachers were least able (or willing) to make a response, her family provided tuition at home. Inclusive teachers are those who take responsibility for responding to diverse learners as the same whilst forcefully putting medical or tragedy models of SEND into abeyance.

Through our own experiences, the authors have come to the conclusion that the journey for SEN needs to be away from the term 'special educational need' and more towards a spectrum of development model. For as long as resourcing is linked to a labelled condition, schools are going to struggle with the battle between philosophy and practice. However, it is through a thorough understanding of each child in a class that a teacher is able to teach. The labels attached to children may indicate a possible set of characteristics but there are as many variations of a particular condition as there are children who have it.

The authors share a view that 'special educational need' is not a helpful term – it identifies children as different, which in turn suggests that pedagogy for these children also needs to be different. The authors have tried to present an argument for a spectrum of provision matched to the spectrum of abilities within a primary setting. They suggest that teaching children with an identified disability is a variant to the 'norm' and not a different proposition. This goes against the notion of 'special'.

Our model – the Spiral Spectrum Model – is offered as a way of viewing this variation without suggesting children with special educational needs are a separate entity, but they exist within a comparative spiral of development. The spiral offers the view that there is not so much a beginning and end in a linear fashion, but that a cohort of children can be compared to each other across the six areas of development. Teachers then plan for this variation, not for a normal group and a special group.

We have not suggested that this is the only way to view the teaching of children with SEN, but that it offers a new perspective fitting with our philosophy of abilities rather than disabilities, and spectrum rather than subdivisions of children. We hope that you find your continued journey to inclusion a revealing and enlightening one!

Additional resources for Part Two

www.headssupportservice.co.uk/wp-content/uploads/2011/04/teachers-standards-2012.pdf
Teachers' Standards 2012.

www.nhs.uk
For outlines of disabilities and conditions.

www.gov.uk
Statistics related to GCSE outcomes.

http://montessori.edu/
The International Montessori Index.

www.steinerwaldorf.org/
The Steiner Waldorf Schools Fellowship.

Trussler, S. (2012) *Special Educational Needs and Primary Initial Teacher Education: Student Learning Experiences in School and University College.* Milton Keynes: Open University.

REFERENCES

Ainscow, M. (2008) 'Developing inclusive education systems: what are the levers for change?', in P. Hick and G. Thomas (eds.) *Inclusion and Diversity in Education*, volume two. London: Sage. pp. 1–13.

Alborz, A., Pearson, D., Farrell, P. and Howes, A. (2009) '*The Impact of Adult Support Staff on Pupils and Mainstream Schools*' (technical report). London: EPPI-Centre, Social Science Research Unit, Institute of Education, University of London.

Allan, J. (2008) *Rethinking Inclusive Education: The Philosophers of Difference in Practice*. Dortrecht: Springer.

Alliance for Inclusive Education (2014) Alliance for Inclusie Education's Campaigns Briefing: February, 2014. Available at: http://www.allfie.org.uk/pages/work/press.html (accessed 31 July 2014).

American Psychiatric Association (2013) *Diagnostic and Statistical Manual of Mental Disorders (DSM-5)* (5th edn). VA: APA.

Armstrong, A.C., Armstrong, D. and Spandagou, I. (2010) *Inclusive Education: International Policy and Practice*. London: Sage.

Barton, L. (2003) *Inclusive Education and Teacher Education: A Basis for Hope or a Discourse of Delusion?* Inaugural Professorial Lecture, London: London Institute of Education.

Black-Hawkins, K. and Florian, L. (2011) Exploring inclusive pedagogy, *British Educational Research Journal*, 37(5): 813–28.

Black-Hawkins, K., Florian, L., and Rouse, M. (2007) *Achievement and Inclusion in Schools*. Abingdon: Routledge.

Blatchford, P., Webster, R. and Russell, A. (2012) *Challenging the Role and Deployment of Teaching Assistants in Mainstream Schools: The Impact on Schools*. London: Institute of Education, University of London.

Booth, T. and Ainscow, M. (2011) *Index for Inclusion: Developing Learning and Participation in Schools*. Bristol: Centre for Studies in Inclusive Education.

Campbell, J., Gilmore, L. and Cluskelly, M. (2003) Changing student teachers' attitudes towards disability and inclusion, *Journal of Intellectual and Developmental Disability*, 28(4): 369–79.

Corbett, J. (1996) *Bad Mouthing: The Language of Special Needs*. London: Falmer.

Corbett, J. (2001) *Supporting Inclusive Education*. London: Routledge.

Cornwall, J. (2013) What makes an inclusive teacher? Can fish climb trees? Mapping the European Agency profile of inclusive teachers to the English system, *Forum Special Issue: Reconceptualising Local Democracy*, 55(1): 31–44.

Darling-Hammond, L. (2006) Constructing 21st century teacher education. *Journal of Teacher Education*, 57(3): pp. 300–314.

Department for Education (2003) *Every Child Matters*. London: DfE.

Department for Education (2011) *Support and Aspiration: A New Approach to Special Educational Needs and Disability*. London: DfE.

Department for Education (2011) *Teachers' Standards*. London: DfE.

Department for Education (2014) *Statistical First Release: GCSE and Equivalent Attainment by Pupil Characteristics in England 2012/13*. London, DfE.

Department for Education and Skills (1997) *Excellence for All Children: Meeting Special Educational Needs*. London: HMSO.

Department for Education and Skills (1998) *Programme of Action*. London: HMSO.

Department for Education and Skills (2001) *The Code of Practice for the Identification and Assessment of Pupils with Special Educational Needs*. London: DfES.

Department for Education and Skills (2004) *Removing Barriers to Achievement: The Government's Strategy for SEN*. London: HMSO.

Department of Education and Science (1978) *Warnock Committee Report*. London: HMSO.

Deary, I.J., Penke, L. and Johnson, W. (2010) The neuroscience of human intelligence differences. *Nature Reviews Neuroscience*, (11): 201–211.

Elliott, J. and Grigorenko, E.L. (2014) *The Dyslexia Debate*. Cambridge: Cambridge University Press.

Engelbrecht, P. (2013) Teacher education for inclusion, international perspectives, *European Journal of Special Needs Education*, 28(2): 115–18.

Finkelstein, V. (1996) We want to remodel the world, *DAIL magazine* (4 October), Editorial.

Florian, L. (ed.) (2007) *Reimagining Special Education*. London: Sage.

Florian, L. (2010) 'Forward', in C. Forlin (ed.), *Changing Paradigms and Innovative Approaches to Teacher Education for Inclusion*. London: Routledge. pp. xviii–xxi.

Giangreco, M.F. (2007) *Absurdities and realities of special education. The complete digital set* [CD]. Thousand Oaks, CA: SAGE/Corwin Press.

Glenny, G.T. (2005) 'Thinking about inclusion', in M. Nind, K. Sheehy, K. Simmons and J. Rix (eds), *Ethics and Research in Inclusive Education: Values into Practice*. Oxon: RoutledgeFalmer. pp. 103–25.

Hart, S. (1996) *Beyond Special Needs: Enhancing Children's Learning through Innovative Thinking*. London: Paul Chapman.

Hart, S., Dixon, A., Drummond, M.J. and McIntyre, D. (2004) *Learning Without Limits*. Maidenhead: Open University Press.

HMSO (1913) *Mental Deficiency Act* (Act of Parliament edn). London: HMSO.

HMSO (1944) *Education Act*. London: HMSO.

HMSO (1970) *Education (Handicapped Children) Act.* London: HMSO.

HMSO (1981) *Education Act.* London: HMSO.

HMSO (2001) *Special Educational Needs and Disability Act.* London: HMSO.

HMSO (2014) *Children and Families Bill* (Law edn). London: England.

Jordan, A., Schwartz, E. and McGhie-Richmond, B. (2009) Preparing teachers for inclusive classrooms, *Teaching and Teacher Education:* 535–42.

Jordan, R. (2005) 'Autistic spectrum disorder', in A. Lewis and B. Norwich (eds), *Special Teaching for Special Children? Pedagogies for Inclusion.* Maidenhead: Open University Press. pp. 110–22.

Jordan, R. and Jones, G. (2012) *Meeting the Needs of Children with Autistic Spectrum Disorders.* London: Routledge.

Kearney, A. (2007) 'Exclusion at school: what is happening for disabled students?', *7th International Conference on Diversity in Organisations, Communities and Nations,* July, Amsterdam.

Lambe, J. and Bones, R. (2006) Student teachers' perceptions about inclusive classroom teaching in Northern Ireland prior to teaching practice experiences, *European Journal of Special Needs Education,* 21(2): 167–86.

Lewis, A. and Norwich, B. (2005) *Special Teaching for Special Children: Pedagogies for Inclusion.* Maidenhead: Open University Press.

Liasidou, A. (2012) *Inclusive Education, Politics and Policy Making.* London: Continuum.

Marks, R. (2013) 'The blue table means you don't have a clue': the persistence of fixed-ability thinking and practices in primary mathematics in English schools, *Forum Special Issue: Reconceptualising Local Democracy,* 55(1): 31–44.

Nind, M., Wearmouth, J., Collins, J., Hall, K., Rix, J. and Sheehy, K. (2004) 'A systematic review of pedagogical approaches that can effectively include children with special educational needs in mainstream classrooms with a particular focus on peer group interactive approaches'. London: EPPI-Centre, Social Science Research Unit, Institute of Education, University of London.

Norwich, B. (2008) *Dilemma of Difference, Inclusion and Disability: International Perspectives and Future Directions.* Oxon: Routledge.

Ofsted (2000) *Evaluating Educational Inclusion: Guidance for Inspectors and Schools.* London: Ofsted.

Ofsted (2011) *The Framework for School Inspections from 2012: An Introduction.* Manchester: Ofsted.

Oliver, M. (2000) 'Profile', in B. Clough and J. Corbett (eds), *Theories of Inclusive Education: A Students' Guide.* London: Paul Chapman. pp. 5–14.

Parry, J., Nind, M. and Sheehy, K. (2010) 'Origins of the social model', in The E214 Team (eds), *E214: Equality, Participation and Inclusion: Learning from Each Other: Block 1: Principles.* Milton Keynes: Open University Press. pp. 101–81.

Pass, S. (2004) *Parallel Paths to Constructivism: Jean Piaget and Lev Vygotsky.* Charlotte, NC: Information Age Publishing Inc.

Peer, L. and Reid, G. (2012) *Special Educational Needs: A Guide for Inclusive Practice.* London: Sage.

Reid, G. (2005) 'Dyslexia', in A. Lewis and B. Norwich (eds), *Special Teaching for Special Children? Pedagogies for Inclusion*. Maidenhead: Open University. pp. 138–49.

Reid, G. (2011) *Dyslexia*. London: Continuum.

Riddick, B. (2012) 'Labelling learners with SEND, the good the bad and the "ugly"', in D. Armstrong and G. Squires (eds), *Contemporary Issues in Special Educational Needs: Considering the Whole Child*. Maidenhead: Open University Press. pp. 56–67.

Rieser, R. (2001) Does language matter?, *Inclusion Now*, 2 (Summer): 16–17.

Rix, J., Hall, K., Nind, M., Sheehy, K. and Wearmouth, J. (2006) *A Systematic Review of Interactions in Pedagogical Approaches with Reported Outcomes for the Academic and Social Inclusion of Pupils with Special Educational Needs* (technical report). London: EPPI-Centre Social Science Research Unit, Institute of Education, University of London.

Robinson, D. (2014) *Developing Initial Teacher Education for Special Educational Needs, Disability and Inclusive Practices*. Unpublished thesis. Milton Keynes: Open University.

Sarason, S. (1990) *The Predictable Failure of Educational Reform: Can We Change Course Before It's Too Late?* San Francisco, CA: Jossey-Bass.

Sautner, S. (2008) Inclusive, safe and caring schools: connecting factors, *Developmental Disabilities Bulletin*, 36(1–2): 135–67.

Slee, R. (2010) 'Political economy, inclusive education and teacher education', in C. Forlin (ed.), *Changing Paradigms and Innovative Approaches in Teacher Education for Inclusion*. London: Routledge. pp. 13–22.

Thomas, G. and Glenny, G. (2005) 'Thinking about inclusion; what reason, what evidence?', in K. Sheehy, M. Nind, J. Rix and K. Simmons (eds), *Ethics and Research in Inclusive Education: Values into Practice*. Oxon: Routledge Falmer. pp. 10–25.

Trussler, S. (2011) *Special Educational Needs and Primary Initial Teacher Education: Student Learning Experiences in School and University College*. Unpublished thesis. Milton Keynes: Open University.

Tucker-Drob, E.M., Briley, D.A. and Harden, K.P. (2013) Genetic and environmental influences on cognition across development and context, *Current Directions in Psychological Science*, 22(5): 349–55.

UNESCO (2009) *Policy Guidelines on Inclusion in Education*. Paris: UNESCO.

Villa, R. and Thousand, V. (2005) *Creating an Inclusive School*. VA: Alexandria.

INDEX